SONGS OF AMERICA

BY JON MEACHAM

Songs of America: Patriotism, Protest, and the Music That Made a Nation
The Soul of America: The Battle for Our Better Angels
Destiny and Power: The American Odyssey of George Herbert Walker Bush
Thomas Jefferson: The Art of Power
American Lion: Andrew Jackson in the White House
American Gospel: God, the Founding Fathers, and the Making of a Nation
Franklin and Winston: An Intimate Portrait of an Epic Friendship
Voices in Our Blood: America's Best on the Civil Rights Movement (editor)

BY TIM McGRAW

STUDIO ALBUMS

Tim McGraw
Not a Moment Too Soon
All I Want
Everywhere
A Place in the Sun
Set This Circus Down
Tim McGraw and the Dancehall Doctors
Live Like You Were Dying
Let It Go
Southern Voice
Emotional Traffic
Two Lanes of Freedom
Sundown Heaven Town
Damn Country Music
Here on Earth

BOOKS

Tim McGraw and the Dancehall Doctors: This Is Ours
My Little Girl (with Tom Douglas)
Love Your Heart (with Tom Douglas)
Humble & Kind
Grit & Grace: Train the Mind, Train the Body, Own Your Life

JON MEACHAM & TIM McGRAW

SONGS OF AMERICA

★ YOUNG READERS EDITION ★

PATRIOTISM, PROTEST, AND THE MUSIC THAT MADE A NATION

DELACORTE PRESS

Text copyright © 2019 by Project #268866, Inc., and Merewether LLC

All rights reserved. Published in the United States by Delacorte Press, an imprint of Random House Children's Books, a division of Penguin Random House LLC, New York.

This work is based on *Songs of America: Patriotism, Protest, and the Music That Made a Nation,* published in hardcover by Random House, a division of Penguin Random House LLC, New York, in 2019.

Delacorte Press is a registered trademark and the colophon is a trademark of Penguin Random House LLC.

Image credits can be found on page 223.
Song lyric credits can be found on page 227.

Visit us on the Web! rhcbooks.com

Educators and librarians, for a variety of teaching tools, visit us at RHTeachersLibrarians.com

Library of Congress Cataloging-in-Publication Data is available upon request.
ISBN 978-0-593-17879-9 (trade) — ISBN 978-0-593-48496-8 (lib. bdg.) — ISBN 978-0-593-17881-2 (ebook)

The text of this book is set in 11.5-point Gamma ITC Std.
Interior design by Cathy Bobak
Jacket art used under license from Shutterstock.com.

MANUFACTURED IN ITALY
10 9 8 7 6 5 4 3 2 1
First Edition

To Keith and Faith,
Mississippi Women

A patriotic song is an enchanted key to memory's deepest cells; it touches secret springs, it kindles sacred flames in chambers of the soul unvisited by other agencies. It wakes to life ten thousand slumbering chords and makes them thrill and pulsate—just as if some loving angel's finger touched them—to that grand God-given sentiment of liberty.

—ELIAS NASON, nineteenth-century American composer

I, too, sing America.

—LANGSTON HUGHES

CONTENTS

A NOTE TO THE READER

In the following pages, Jon Meacham wrote the narrative text that takes the American story, with special reference to music that shaped those years, from the period before the Revolutionary War through the attacks of Tuesday, September 11, 2001, and the election of Barack Obama as the forty-fourth president of the United States. We occasionally drew on Meacham's previous works of history and journalism, including his books about Thomas Jefferson, Andrew Jackson, Franklin Roosevelt, and Winston Churchill, and the more general *The Soul of America,* as well as essays of his first published in the *New York Times, Time, Newsweek,* and *Vanity Fair.*

Writing from his perspective as an artist and performer, Tim McGraw offers his take on selected songs in a series of sidebars. No effort has been made to be encyclopedic; readers will surely argue with us about why one song was included but another wasn't. So be it: We welcome open—and open-hearted—debate.

It's our hope that *Songs of America* is the opening, not the closing, act in a conversation about the nation's diversity and complexity. For that's among the reasons we undertook the project: to inspire Americans to think more widely and more deeply about the country Abraham Lincoln called "the last best hope of earth."

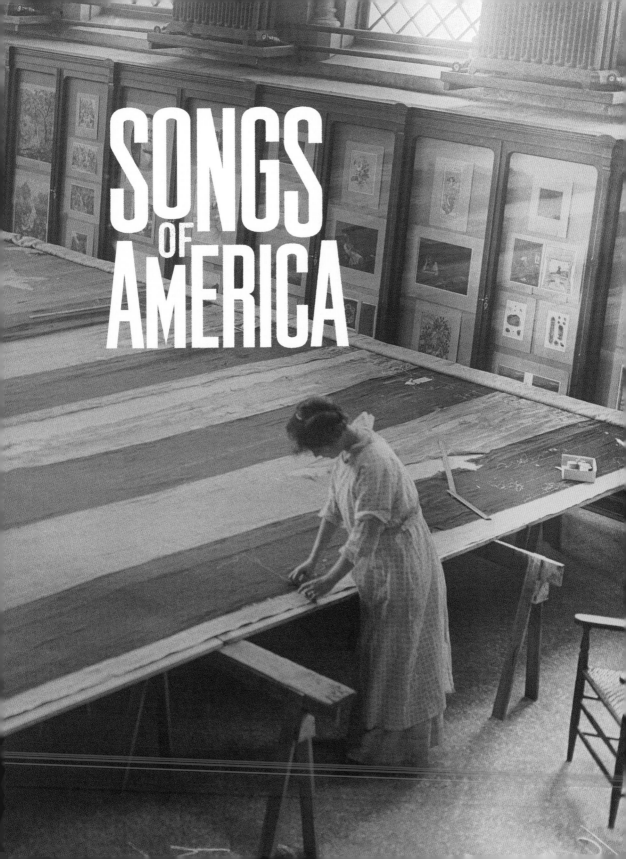

SONGS
OF
AMERICA

THE MUSIC OF HISTORY

> Nothing is more agreeable, and ornamental, than good music; every officer, for the credit of his corps, should take care to provide it.
>
> —GEORGE WASHINGTON

In the beginning were the words—the stately rhythms of the Declaration of Independence, the passionate eloquence of Thomas Paine's *Common Sense,* the steady notes of the Constitution. All men, Thomas Jefferson asserted, were created equal, with unalienable rights to life, liberty, and the pursuit of happiness. In building such a nation, we, in Paine's stirring prose, had it in our power to begin the world over again. And that enterprise would, as the Constitution's preamble put it, have a central, consuming aim: a more perfect union.

History isn't just something we read; it's also something we *hear.* We hear the musketry on the green at Lexington and Concord and the hoofbeats of Paul Revere's midnight ride. We hear the moans of the wounded and of the dying on the fields of Antietam and of Gettysburg, the quiet clump of the boots of Grant and Lee on the porch steps of Wilmer McLean's house at Appomattox—and the crack of a pistol at Ford's Theatre. We hear the cries of the enslaved, the pleas of suffragists, the surf at Omaha Beach. We hear a sonorous president, his voice scratchy on the radio, reassuring us that the only thing we have to fear is fear

American revolutionaries on the march in the painting
The Nation Makers, by Howard Pyle.

itself; and we hear another president, impossibly young and dashing, his breath white in the inaugural air, telling us to ask not what our country can do for us but what we can do for our country. And we hear the whoosh of helicopters in the distant jungles of Southeast Asia and the baritone of a minister, standing before the Lincoln Memorial, telling us about his dream.

Such are the sounds of our history.

And through it all, through all the years of strife, we've been shaped not only by our words and our deeds but also by our music, by the lyrics and the instrumentals that have carried us through dark days and enabled us to celebrate bright ones.

The paramount role of music in life and in the lives of nations has the deepest of roots. Plato and Aristotle wrote of its centrality to the formation of noble human souls and of civilized society; Newton and Shakespeare saw the universe in terms of the harmony—or disharmony—of the spheres; and in the eighteenth-century Age of Enlightenment, the Scottish writer and politician Andrew Fletcher brilliantly linked music and civic life, writing, "I knew a very wise man . . . [who] believed if a man were permitted to make all the ballads, he need not care who should make the laws of a nation." One way to gain a fuller understanding of our confounding nation is to explore the music of patriotism, which is also, inevitably, the music of protest. To us, patriotism celebrates and commemorates; protest critiques and corrects. The two are inextricably intertwined and are as vital to each other as wings to a bird, for the nation cannot soar without both.

A true patriot salutes the flag but always makes sure it's flying over a nation that's not only free but fair, not only strong but just. History and reason summon us to embrace love and loyalty—to a citizenship that seeks a better world. What, really, could be more patriotic than that? What, in the end, could be more *American*?

That's our mission now: to hear the music that has lifted us from danger, kept us together amid tragedy, united us anew in triumph, and urged us on toward justice. From our earliest times to our latest, we hear not only the spoken but the sung word, and the music of the nation reminds us where we've been, who we are—and what we can become.

CHAPTER ONE

THE SENSATIONS OF FREEDOM

By uniting we stand, by dividing we fall.
—JOHN DICKINSON, "The Liberty Song," 1768

Objects of the most stupendous magnitude, measures in which the lives and liberties of millions, born and unborn, are most essentially interested, are now before us. We are in the very midst of a Revolution, the most complete, unexpected, and remarkable of any in the history of nations.
—JOHN ADAMS, Sunday, June 9, 1776

Remember the Ladies.
—ABIGAIL ADAMS, to her husband as the Founders debated independence

A s daylight faded on Friday, June 10, 1768, officials of the British Crown stepped across the wharves of Boston Harbor to seize the *Liberty,* a sloop owned by the merchant John Hancock of Massachusetts. The charge: that Hancock's men had smuggled casks of Madeira wine from the *Liberty*'s hold to avoid paying stiff duties recently imposed under the hated Townshend Acts. Anticipating trouble, the imperial authorities had deployed the heavily armed warship HMS *Romney*— which contemporaries described as a "fine new 50-Gun ship"—for the task. "This conduct provoked the People, who had collected on the Shore," the *Boston Gazette* reported, and the gathering of colonials surged toward the British collector of customs, Joseph Harrison, as he came back off the *Liberty.* On the street

"We hold these truths": Franklin, Adams, and Jefferson at work on the Declaration of Independence.

adjoining the harbor, Harrison wrote, "we were pursued by the Mob which by this time was increased to a great multitude. The onset was begun by throwing dirt at me, which was presently succeeded by volleys of stones, brickbats, sticks, or anything that came to hand. . . . About this time I received a violent blow on the breast . . . and I verily believe that if I had fallen, I should never have got up again, the People to all appearance being determined on blood and murder."

The royal governor of Massachusetts was flummoxed, denouncing what he called this "Great Riot" in dispatches to London. The colonials, naturally, had a different view. To them, the specter of the *Romney* taking control of Hancock's *Liberty* was an outrage, a veritable act of war. "We will support our liberties," a patriot leader cried after the seizure, "depending upon the strength of our own arms and God."

Hearing the news, John Dickinson of Pennsylvania was moved to pick up his pen to strike a blow in favor of the colonial cause. Born in 1732, raised in Dover, Delaware, and trained as a lawyer in Philadelphia and at the Middle Temple in London, Dickinson had recently published an influential series of essays entitled *Letters from a Farmer in Pennsylvania, to the Inhabitants of the British Colonies.* The Townshend Acts had been the occasion for Dickinson's *Letters;* in Boston, Joseph Harrison had found Dickinson's writings "inflaming and seditious . . . tending to poison and incense the minds of the people and alienate them from all regard and obedience to the Legislature of the Mother Country."

A sustained attempt to argue for the justice of the colonial view that representation was a civil right in the English tradition, the *Letters* would bring Dickinson acclaim. "From infancy," Dickinson had written, "I was taught to love liberty and humanity."

His *Letters* had been prose. Now, in the wake of the clash in Boston, he would try poetry, composing a series of verses in honor of the resistance in Massachusetts. "I enclose you a song for American freedom," Dickinson wrote James Otis of Boston. He told Otis that Arthur Lee of Virginia, a Dickinson friend, had contributed eight lines of "The Liberty Song." Published in Philadelphia and in the *Boston Gazette* of July 18, 1768, the song was set to William Boyce's "Heart of Oak," a patriotic British number popular with the Royal Navy.

> Come join hand in hand, brave Americans all,
> And rouse your bold hearts at fair Liberty's call;
> No tyrannous acts shall suppress your just claim,
> Or stain with dishonor America's name.
>
> In freedom we're born, and in freedom we'll live;
> Our purses are ready,
> Steady, Friends, steady,
> Not as slaves, but as freemen our money we'll give.
>
> Our worthy forefathers—let's give them a cheer—
> To climates unknown did courageously steer;
> Thro' oceans, to deserts, for freedom they came,
> And, dying, bequeath'd us their freedom and fame.
>
> Their generous bosoms all dangers despis'd,
> So highly, so wisely, their birthrights they priz'd;
> We'll keep what they gave, we will piously keep,
> Nor frustrate their toils on the land and the deep.
>
> The Tree, their own hands had to Liberty rear'd,
> They lived to behold growing strong and rever'd;
> With transport they cry'd, "Now our wishes we gain,
> For our children shall gather the fruits of our pain."

Swarms of placemen and pensioners soon will appear,

Like locusts deforming the charms of the year;

Suns vainly will rise, showers vainly descend,

If we are to drudge for what others shall spend.

Then join hand in hand brave Americans all,

By uniting we stand, by dividing we fall;

In so righteous a cause let us hope to succeed,

For Heaven approves of each generous deed.

All ages shall speak with amaze and applause,

Of the courage we'll show in support of our laws;

To die we can bear—but to serve we disdain,

For shame is to freedom more dreadful than pain.

This bumper I crown for our sovereign's health,

And this for Britannia's glory and wealth;

That wealth and that glory immortal may be,

If she is but just—and if we are but free.

Dickinson had great hopes for his work. His language was designed to appeal to the emotions of his broad audience. "By uniting we stand, by dividing we fall"; "In so righteous a cause let us hope to succeed"; "To die we can bear—but to serve we disdain"—the song's message was unmistakable. Unity was all; a common cause would carry the day; the stakes could not be higher.

Here, in the middle of the summer of 1768, eight years before the Declaration of Independence, an American patriot was making a popular case for American identity and for American action in the more universal and stirring genre of music. "The Liberty Song" quickly spread. To John Adams, Dickinson had done something wondrous. "This," Adams remarked of the song, "is cultivating the sensations of freedom."

THE LIBERTY SONG

I was struck by the melody and structure of this song. We don't really think of the Revolution in terms of music, except maybe "Yankee Doodle Dandy." But John Dickinson's words, together with the older British music, create something uplifting and empowering. Having strong rhythm, it would be classified as a march, with around 120 beats per minute. The irony of the choice of the music of the British anthem isn't lost on me—it's shrewd to put new words to an old tune, especially if you're trying to turn the familiar on its head. What really speaks to me is this verse:

> All ages shall speak with amaze and applause,
> Of the courage we'll show in support of our laws;
> To die we can bear—but to serve we disdain,
> For shame is to freedom more dreadful than pain.

Dickinson clearly understands that this is a moment in time that will live on forever (at least he's hoping it will, and hope drives so much of art), and he used this idea to inspire real people to take real steps toward independence—and transformation. —T.M.

Yet America did not declare its independence in the wake of Dickinson's song, or for eight years afterward. The ensuing period was marked by further taxes and protests, more debate over the nature of representative government, and rising concerns over the role of imperial authority in colonial affairs. How did a group of disparate British North Americans, subjects of the British Empire all their lives, decide to risk everything?

The nation was an experiment—and a risky one at that. Nobody knew if the Revolutionary War would succeed; it has been said that the Founders joked, mordantly, about how they had to hang together or they would surely hang separately.

Parliament's imposition of the Stamp Act—a tax on paper goods—provoked colonial resistance and helped create revolutionary sentiment.

A pattern took hold. The British Parliament imposed new taxes to raise revenue from British America. Colonists in their sundry capitals (Boston, Annapolis, Philadelphia, Williamsburg, and so on) resisted. The royal governments in the New World and the establishment in Britain grew impatient with what they saw as a continent populated by the recalcitrant, the unreasonable, and the ungrateful.

In these years Americans played and hummed and sang different versions of "Yankee Doodle Dandy," with its sprightly rhythm; they recited, too, ballads like 1775's "The Pennsylvania Song":

> We'll not give up our birthright,
> Our foes shall find us men;
> As good as they, in any shape,
> The British troops shall ken.
>
> Huzza! Brave boys, we'll beat them
> On any hostile plain;
> For freedom, wives, and children dear,
> The battle we'll maintain.
>
> What! Can those British tyrants think,
> Our fathers cross'd the main,
> And savage foes, and dangers met,
> To be enslav'd by them?
>
> If so, they are mistaken,
> For we will rather die;
> And since they have become our foes,
> Their forces we defy.
>
> And all the world shall know,
> Americans are free,
> Nor slaves nor cowards we will prove,
> Great Britain soon shall see.

"The Liberty Song," "Yankee Doodle Dandy," and "The Pennsylvania Song" were patriot favorites to sing on the battlefield.

The idea of an American "birthright" expressed in these verses was a prevalent one. The American revolutionaries took the positions they did—positions that led to the Declaration of Independence in 1776—partly because they saw themselves as Englishmen who were being denied a full share of the benefits of English life. Every proposal from London, every thought of a tax, every sign of imperial authority, raised fears of tyranny in America, for as Englishmen they were intuitively on guard against any encroachment on their liberty.

Still, in the summer of 1775, the independence-minded colonists were not ready to fight a total war, dispatching an "Olive Branch Petition" to London, addressed directly to George III. The king refused to receive it and had in the meantime issued a hawkish "Proclamation for Suppressing Rebellion and Sedition," asserting that the Americans were in "open and avowed rebellion." This was a serious blow to those seeking reconciliation of some kind with the mother country.

As 1776 dawned, Thomas Paine published *Common Sense,* a wildly bestselling pamphlet making the case for independence. "The cause of America is," Paine wrote, "in a great measure, the cause of all mankind." His words had remarkable resonance. "Its effects were sudden and extensive upon the American mind," the patriot-physician Benjamin Rush recalled. "It was read by public men, repeated in clubs, spouted in schools, and in one instance, delivered from the pulpit instead of a sermon." In Connecticut, an appreciative reader wrote, "We were blind, but on reading these enlightening words, the scales have fallen from our eyes." George Washington praised Paine's "unanswerable reasoning."

As his subjects absorbed Paine's arguments for a new era in democratic government, George III was brokering treaties with European powers to enlist soldiers for service in the New World—treaties that were leaked to American newspapers, alarming the colonists. There was terrible military news from Canada and fears that the British were about to strike the Atlantic coast from Nova Scotia. For the more forward-leaning Americans, the answer was to declare independence, seek an alliance with France, and risk all in a bold bid for nationhood and for liberty.

On Monday, July 1, 1776, Dickinson rose in the Congress to argue that the Americans should wait to see if it was certain that France would enter the war on the side of the new nation before making the final break with Britain. It was an eminently reasonable position, one that in any other month of the crisis might well have prevailed. Yet this time it did not. By Tuesday, July 2, the decision was unanimous: The Declaration of Independence was to be adopted. "Yesterday," John Adams wrote his wife, Abigail, on Wednesday, July 3, 1776, "the greatest question was decided which ever was debated in America; and a greater perhaps never was, nor will be, decided among men." Adams was hearing history's trumpets. "The second day of July, 1776, will be the most memorable epoch in the history of America," he added. "I am apt to believe that it will be celebrated by succeeding generations as the great anniversary festival. It ought to be commemorated as the day of deliverance, by solemn acts of devotion to God Almighty. It ought to be solemnized with pomp and parade, with shows, games, sports, guns, bells, bonfires, and illuminations, from one end of this continent to the other, from this time forward forevermore." The fourth, not the second, would ultimately be the festival date, but Adams's sentiments were exactly right.

The words of the Declaration of Independence are among the most hallowed ever rendered in English. Washington recognized their significance from the beginning, ordering the Continental Army to muster its brigades to hear the cadences of the declaration as they marched to war.

The preamble met the moment. "We hold these truths to be self-evident," Jefferson wrote, "that all men are created equal; that they are endowed by their creator with certain unalienable rights; that among these are life, liberty & the pursuit of happiness: that to secure these rights, governments are instituted among men, deriving their just powers from the consent of the governed; that

John Trumbull's rendering of the signing of the Declaration of Independence in Philadelphia on Thursday, July 4, 1776.

whenever any form of government becomes destructive of these ends, it is the right of the people to alter or to abolish it, & to institute new government, laying its foundation on such principles, & organizing its powers in such form, as to them shall seem most likely to effect their safety & happiness."

America was founded, then, on an idea—one not fully realized even now, but still an idea worth pondering and, more to the point, pursuing.

In that spirit, Jefferson's language in the declaration evoked not fear but hope, a fact long recognized by those who followed the Founders in the work of governing the United States.

"All honor to Jefferson," Lincoln would say of the flawed but brilliant architect of the American promise.

Dour but devoted, John Adams believed America was worth all the "toil and blood and treasure" it would cost to build.

The "whole . . . Audience broke forth in the Chorus," Abigail Adams wrote of hearing "Hail Columbia" for the first time.

* * *

The odyssey begun by the declaration was carried forward by the Constitution that was drafted in the summer of 1787—a constitution that took account of ambition and appetite. "If men were angels," James Madison had written in *The Federalist Papers*, "no government would be necessary"—and given that men were so self-evidently unangelic, the American government was designed to check our passions and balance our failings. "The essence of a free government consists in an effectual control of rivalries," John Adams wrote. "The executive and the legislative powers are natural rivals; and if each has not an effectual control over the other, the weaker will ever be the lamb in the paws of the wolf. The nation which will not adopt an equilibrium of power must adopt a despotism. There is no other alternative. Rivalries must be controlled, or they will throw all things into confusion; and there is nothing but despotism or a balance of power which can control them."

By the time of the Revolutionary War, many Americans were used to hearing the political and the temporal framed in terms of the eternal and the absolute. "We have incontestable evidence that God Almighty, with all the powers of heaven, are on our side," Samuel Sherwood, a Connecticut pastor and kinsman of Aaron Burr, said. "Great numbers of angels, no doubt, are encamping round our coast, for our defense and protection. Michael stands ready, with all the artillery of heaven, to encounter the [British] dragon, and to vanquish this black host." Entitled *The Church's Flight into the Wilderness: An Address on the Times,* Sherwood's sermon was preached the same month Paine published *Common Sense.*

As the late Columbia University scholar Robert A. Ferguson argued, many Americans also saw the cause for self-government as one allied with the forces of enlightenment—revolutionary victories were triumphs of right reason against discredited notions of the immutable authority of princes and prelates—and saw

America as the living embodiment of Enlightenment ideals. "Education, exploration, and invention should unite in the general advance of humanity, but that possibility depends upon prompt action in the more immediate and unpredictable realm of politics," Ferguson wrote. "Progress, in other words, is not a predetermined evolution through fixed stages of history."

A commonly cited example of the Enlightenment-era nature of the American experience comes from Jefferson: "All eyes are opened, or opening, to the rights of man. The general spread of the light of science has already laid open to every view the palpable truth, that the mass of mankind has not been born with saddles on their backs, nor a favored few booted and spurred, ready to ride them legitimately, by the grace of God."

Yet a country created to liberate chose to subjugate women, enslave African Americans, and persecute indigenous peoples; much of the work of the ensuing centuries would be the difficult fight to apply the words of Jefferson in the declaration not just to *some* but to *all*.

The arguments about inclusion were older than the republic itself. A few months before the Second Continental Congress broke decisively with Great Britain, John Adams was at work in Philadelphia when he received an engaging letter from Abigail. "I long to hear that you have declared an independency—and by the way in the new Code of Laws which I suppose it will be necessary for you to make I desire you would Remember the Ladies, and be more generous and favorable to them than your ancestors," Mrs. Adams wrote. "Do not put such unlimited power into the hands of the Husbands. Remember all Men would be tyrants if they could. If particular care and attention is not paid to the Ladies we are determined to foment a Rebellion, and will not hold ourselves bound by any Laws in which we have no voice, or Representation."

Twenty years on, the *Philadelphia Minerva* of Saturday, October 17, 1795, published a song in line with Mrs. Adams's sentiments. (The verses had first appeared in print in April 1795 in the *Weekly Museum,* a New York magazine.) Set to the tune of "God Save the King," it was called "Rights of Woman":

> GOD save each Female's right,
> Show to her ravish'd sight
> Woman is Free;
> Let Freedom's voice prevail . . .
>
> Let Woman have a share,
> Nor yield to slavish fear,
> Her equal rights declare,
> And well maintain.
>
> A voice re-echoing round,
> With joyful accents sound,
> "Woman is Free;
> Assert the noble claim,
> All selfish arts disdain;"
> Hark how the note proclaim,
> "Woman is Free!"

But of course women weren't, and neither were Black people. Among the most important literary voices in early America was Phillis Wheatley, an African-born woman who was sold into slavery and arrived in Massachusetts in 1761, when she was about eight. Educated by her owners, John and Susanna Wheatley, Phillis Wheatley was precocious and began writing verse at around age twelve. In a 1775 poem titled "To His Excellency George Washington," Wheatley introduced the notion of America as what the scholar Thomas J. Steele called a "fully developed personification" of the goddess Columbia:

> Celestial choir! enthron'd in realms of light,
> Columbia's scenes of glorious toils I write.
> While freedom's cause her anxious breast alarms,
> She flashes dreadful in refulgent arms.
> See mother earth her offspring's fate bemoan,
> And nations gaze at scenes before unknown!
> See the bright beams of heaven's revolving light
> Involved in sorrows and the veil of night! . . .
>
> Proceed, great chief, with virtue on thy side,
> Thy ev'ry action let the Goddess guide.

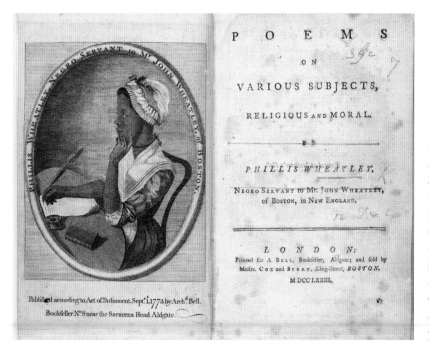

Phillis Wheatley's *Poems on Various Subjects, Religious and Moral,* published in 1773; George Washington praised her "genius," and Benjamin Rush wrote that her verses "not only do honor to her sex, but to human nature."

> A crown, a mansion, and a throne that shine,
> With gold unfading, *Washington*! Be thine.

She sent the verses to Washington, then in the field, who read them with gratitude. "I thank you most sincerely for your polite notice of me, in the elegant Lines you enclosed; and however undeserving I may be of such encomium and panegyric, the style and manner exhibit a striking proof of your great poetical Talents," Washington wrote Wheatley from Cambridge in February 1776. (The poem found its way into the *Pennsylvania Magazine* after Washington sent it to a friend who arranged its publication.) Washington invited Wheatley to call on him, telling her that he would "be happy to see a person so favoured by the Muses, and to whom nature has been so liberal and beneficent in her dispensations."

A devout Christian, Wheatley broached then-verboten notions of equality. In her "On Being Brought from Africa to America," she wrote:

> Remember, *Christians, Negros,* black as *Cain,*
> May be refin'd, and join th' angelic train.

When she turned her attention to the nation at large, Wheatley wrote of America as a sublime experiment:

> *Lo!* Freedom comes. Th' prescient Muse foretold,
> All Eyes th' accomplish'd Prophecy behold:
> Her Port describ'd, *"She moves divinely fair,*
> *Olive and Laurel bind her golden Hair."*
> She, the bright Progeny of Heaven, descends,
> And every Grace her sovereign Step attends;
> For now kind Heaven, indulgent to our Prayer,

In smiling *Peace* resolves the Din of *War.*
Fix'd in *Columbia* her illustrious Line,
And bids in thee her future Councils shine.
To every Realm her Portals open'd wide,
Receives from each the full commercial Tide.
Each Art and Science now with rising Charms
Th' expanding Heart with Emulation warms.
E'en great *Britannia* sees with dread Surprize,
And from the dazzling Splendor turns her Eyes! . . .

Auspicious Heaven shall fill with fav'ring Gales,
Where e'er *Columbia* spreads her swelling Sails:
To every Realm shall *Peace* her Charms display,
And Heavenly *Freedom* spread her golden Ray.

Voices of reform and of inclusion and of nobility could be heard, then, but were little heeded.

From the moment everything came together, everything seemed to be falling apart. Initially hailed as a hero, President Washington soon became a figure of partisan strife as the nation divided into two competing factions—the Federalists, led by Washington, Alexander Hamilton, and Adams, and the Republicans, led by Jefferson and Madison.

Naïvely, perhaps, the early leaders of the republic had professed a belief that partisanship could be banished from political life. Washington was to warn the country of what he called "the baneful effects of the spirit of party."

He knew of what he spoke. His eight years as president were riven with partisan warfare as each side, believing the other possibly fatal to the American experiment, fought openly and covertly to thwart and even destroy the other. Whether the issue was the country's relations with England and with France, finance and the distribution of powers, or simply the ceremonial aspects of the presidency itself, Federalists and Republicans engaged in ferocious fighting. Such partisan battling, Washington wrote in 1796, "agitates the community with ill-founded jealousies and false alarms, kindles the animosity of one part against another, foments occasionally riot and insurrection. It opens the door to foreign influence and corruption, which finds a facilitated access to the government itself through the channels of party passions."

In 1798, at an hour of war fever that had led to the passage of the Alien and Sedition Acts—designed by Federalists, in part, to enable them to suppress even legitimate political opposition—the kind of party feeling Washington had deplored was pervasive and defining. England and France were at war, and both nations were pressuring the United States to join the fight. Republicans in particular were anxious to support, or at least not actively oppose, the French, who were then in the midst of their own revolution.

The politics of the moment found expression in song. The Federalist ode "Adams and Liberty," by Robert Treat Paine, Jr., was published in 1798 and was sung to the tune of "To Anacreon in Heaven," an old English club song, as a way for the president's supporters to claim that they, not the Jeffersonian Republicans, were the true Americans:

> Ye sons of Columbia, who bravely have fought,
> For those rights, which unstained from your Sires had descended,
> May you long taste the blessings your valour has brought,
> And your sons reap the soil which their fathers defended.
> 'Mid the reign of mild peace, May your nation increase,
> With the glory of Rome, and the wisdom of Greece;

And ne'er may the sons of Columbia be slaves,
While the earth bears a plant, or the sea rolls its waves . . .
Let Fame to the world sound America's voice;
No intrigue can her sons from their government sever;
Her pride is her Adams; His laws are her choice,
And shall flourish, till Liberty slumber for ever.
Then unite, heart and hand,
Like Leonidas' band,
And swear to the God of the ocean and land;
That ne'er shall the sons of Columbia be slaves,
While the earth bears a plant, or the sea rolls its waves.

Nevertheless, Jefferson defeated Adams in the presidential election of 1800, a victory heralded by Jeffersonians as a restoration of the principles of 1776. (Campaigns to make America great again have a long history.) In this partisan view, the heavy Federalist hand was lifted, and what Jefferson had called "the reign of witches" was coming to an end. In his inaugural address on Wednesday, March 4, 1801, the new president spoke of comity amid controversy. "All . . . will bear in mind this sacred principle, that though the will of the majority is in all cases to prevail, that will to be rightful must be reasonable; that the minority possess their equal rights, which equal law must protect, and to violate would be oppression," Jefferson said. "Let us, then, fellow-citizens, unite with one heart and one mind. Let us restore to social intercourse that harmony and affection without which liberty and even life itself are but dreary things." Warm words, but a song sung by his partisans, entitled "Jefferson and Liberty," was sharper in tone:

The gloomy night before us flies,
The reign of Terror now is o'er;
Its Gags, Inquisitors and Spies,

Its herds of harpies are no more
Rejoice! Columbia's Sons, rejoice!
To tyrants never bend the knee,
But join with heart and soul and voice,
For *Jefferson and Liberty.*

So it would go for centuries in American politics—a politics in which freedom of thought and of expression allowed divergent views to contend against one another in what seemed wars without end. That was the price of liberty: The American system was designed for conflict.

"Men have differed in opinion, and been divided into parties by these opinions, from the first origin of societies and in all governments where they have been permitted freely to think and to speak." Jefferson wrote these words in 1813 in a letter to . . . John Adams.

At its best, American public life has moved forward not in moments of total agreement—moments virtually unknown in human experience—but when enough of us have seen that devotion to the ideal of liberty should prevail over our inevitable divisions of opinion. That insight informed one of the most important anthems of the early republic, one written by Joseph Hopkinson, the Philadelphia lawyer and judge, at the height of the 1790s battle between Adams and Jefferson.

At home one Saturday afternoon in April 1798, Hopkinson received an acquaintance—an actor-singer named Gilbert Fox. Fox was starring in a tragedy, *The Italian Monk,* and had advertised a benefit showing. Ticket sales, however, were slow, and Fox was looking for something to revive the box office. "His prospects were very disheartening," Hopkinson recalled, "but he said that if he could get a patriotic song adapted to 'The President's March,' he did not doubt of a full house." Hopkinson agreed to try his hand at the task and set himself to it without delay.

The next day, a Sunday, Fox returned to Hopkinson's and found that his old friend had composed a four-verse ballad, "Hail Columbia," with a memorable chorus: "Firm, united let us be, / Rallying round our liberty, / As a band of brothers joined, / Peace and safety we shall find."

> Hail Columbia! happy land!
> Hail, ye heroes! Heav'n-born band!
> Who fought and bled in freedom's cause,
> Who fought and bled in freedom's cause,
> And when the storm of war was gone
> Enjoy'd the peace your valor won.
> Let independence be our boast,
> Ever mindful what it cost;
> Ever grateful for the prize,
> Let its Altar reach the skies.
>
> Firm, united let us be,
> Rallying round our Liberty,
> As a band of Brothers joined,
> Peace and safety we shall find.
>
> Immortal Patriots, rise once more,
> Defend your rights—defend your shore!
> Let no rude foe, with impious hand,
> Let no rude foe, with impious hand,
> Invade the shrine where sacred lies
> Of toil and blood, the well-earned prize,
> While offering peace, sincere and just,
> In heav'n we place a manly trust,

That truth and justice will prevail,
And every scheme of bondage fail.

Sound, sound the trump of fame,
Let Washington's great name
Ring thro the world with loud applause,
Ring thro the world with loud applause,
Let every clime to Freedom dear,
Listen with a joyful ear,
With equal skill, with Godlike pow'r
He governs in the fearful hour
Of horrid war, or guides with ease
The happier times of honest peace. . . .

Joseph Hopkinson of Philadelphia wrote the unifying "Hail Columbia" in part to combat what Washington called "the baneful effects of the spirit of party."

It was a triumph. Abigail Adams, who was in the theater on the night of its debut, told her sister that "the whole . . . Audience broke forth in the Chorus whilst the thunder from their Hands was incessant, and at the close they rose, gave 3 Huzzas, that you might have heard a mile—My head aches in consequence of it."

The Revolution was rendered as a righteous undertaking carried through by a "Heav'n-born band"; succeeding generations were called, in an echo of Shakespeare, to be a "band of brothers"; and the work of the ages was the promulgation of liberty—"That truth and justice will prevail, / And every scheme of bondage fail."

"Hail Columbia" was considered by many to be *the* national anthem for many years, but a 1931 act of Congress would elevate a different composition to official primacy—a series of lines written about the siege of Fort McHenry, in Maryland, amid a war that's often overlooked but was vital in its day and its way.

CHAPTER TWO

LAND WHERE OUR FATHERS DIED

Who are we? And for what are we going to fight? Are we the titled slaves of George the Third? The military conscripts of Napoleon the Great? Or the frozen peasants of the Russian czar? No, we are the free born sons of America; the citizens of the only republic now existing in the world; and the only people on Earth who possess rights, liberties, and property which they dare call their own.
—ANDREW JACKSON, calling for militia to fight the British, 1812

I looked at my hands to see if I was the same person now that I was free. There was such a glory over everything, the sun came like gold through the trees, and over the fields, and I felt like I was in Heaven.
—HARRIET TUBMAN, on crossing into freedom in 1849

Major George Armistead knew what he wanted. As the Virginia-born officer took command of Fort McHenry in Baltimore Harbor in the summer of 1813, a year into the War of 1812, he wrote his senior officer: "We, Sir, are ready at Fort McHenry to defend Baltimore against invading by the enemy. That is to say, we are ready except that we have no suitable ensign to display . . . and it is my desire to have a flag so large that the British will have no difficulty in seeing it from a distance." It was a bit of swagger, a touch of bombast, a manifestation of pride—and because it was all those things, it was also very American.

Armistead was in luck, for just such a flag had been recently commissioned.

The War of 1812 brought the sacking and burning of Washington, D.C., but ultimately resulted in a greater sense of American identity.

For a fee that came to $405.90, Mary Young Pickersgill of Albemarle Street in Baltimore had agreed to sew a huge (thirty by forty-two feet) Stars and Stripes for Fort McHenry, as well as a storm flag (seventeen by twenty-five feet) for an additional $168.54.

The flags were for a fort that became the focus of a prolonged British attack, on the tumultuous Tuesday and Wednesday of September 13 and 14, 1814. By chance, a Washington lawyer, Francis Scott Key, was in Baltimore to attempt to secure the release of Dr. William Beanes, an American who had been captured by the British. At the time of the bombardment, Key was aboard a sloop in the harbor, and only by keeping an eye out for the colors could he monitor the battle.

It was a long and terrible day in the middle of a war that was itself long and terrible. The war, which lasted from 1812 to early 1815, was a struggle to ratify

Much of the War of 1812 unfolded on the high seas; this is a depiction of the battle between the USS *Constitution* and the British warship *Guerriere*.

the American Revolution. The immediate occasion was resentment over the British impressment of American sailors and concerns over British alliances with indigenous tribes who were seen as threats to white American settlers, but, as the historian Gordon S. Wood wrote, "In the end, many Americans came to believe that they had to fight another war with Great Britain in order to reaffirm their national independence and establish their elusive identity." In many ways, the Revolutionary period did not truly conclude until the Treaty of Ghent and the Battle of New Orleans brought the War of 1812 to a close in 1815. The conflict, sometimes known to contemporaries as "Mr. Madison's War," then, can be seen as a climactic chapter in the saga of the Revolutionary War.

Francis Scott Key was a firsthand witness to one of the critical closing hours of that story. Watching the battle for Fort McHenry—the British attack, under

JACKSON'S VICTORY AT NEW ORLEANS AND DEATH OF GEN- PAKENHAM.

Andrew Jackson's epic victory at New Orleans in the early days of January 1815 propelled "Old Hickory" to national fame, setting the stage for the Age of Jackson.

the command of Vice Admiral Alexander Cochrane, lasted about twenty-five hours—Key was worried, for Baltimore was at risk of suffering the same fate that had struck Washington a few weeks before: a sacking and burning at the hands of the enemy. The British flotilla in the harbor was extraordinary and included the frigates *Seahorse, Surprise, and Severn,* and the "bomb vessels" *Meteor, Devastation, Aetna, Volcano,* and *Terror.* "We were like pigeons tied by the legs to be shot at," Judge Joseph H. Nicholson, who fought under Armistead, wrote. "The men in the fort watched the explosions light up the sky like lightning flashes," Lonn Taylor, Kathleen M. Kendrick, and Jeffrey L. Brodie wrote in a Smithsonian history, *The Star-Spangled Banner.* "Baltimoreans could clearly see the stream of sparks from the bombs' fuses arching through the air. The sounds of a torrential rain, which had worsened during the day, mixed with peals of thunder, which in turn joined the cacophony caused by the mortars, bombs, and rockets."

As Armistead recalled the bombardment, the British fired fifteen to eighteen hundred shells at Fort McHenry. "The only means we had of directing our guns," Armistead wrote in a report to Secretary of War James Monroe, "was by the blaze of their rockets and the flashes of their guns." Reflecting on the attack, Armistead said, "A few of these fell short. A large proportion burst over us, throwing their fragments among us, and threatening destruction. Many passed over, and about four hundred fell within the works." Yet, amazingly, only four Americans were killed, with twenty-four wounded.

Watching from afar—he was on a vessel in Old Roads Bay—Key peered through the mists of dawn and the haze of cannon

The original "Star-Spangled Banner," made by Mary Young Pickersgill of Baltimore.

fire, waiting for enough sunlight to see whether Major Armistead had held his ground.

Then, slowly, the verdict became clear. As Key would write, in verses scribbled on the back of a letter while he was still aboard his sloop, the flag—Mrs. Pickersgill's flag—was there. "As the last vessel spread her canvas to the wind," a British midshipman wrote of the royal forces' withdrawal, "the Americans hoisted a most superb and splendid ensign on their battery, and fired at the same time a gun of defiance."

Key finished his composition at the Indian Queen Hotel in Baltimore, and it was quickly published.

> What so proudly we hail'd at the
>   twilight's last gleaming,
> Whose broad stripes and bright stars
>   through the perilous fight,
> O'er the ramparts we watch'd, were so
>   gallantly streaming?
> And the rockets' red glare, the bombs
>   bursting in air,
> Gave proof through the night that our
>   flag was still there;
> O say does that star-spangled banner
>   yet wave,
> O'er the land of the free and the home
>   of the brave?

Francis Scott Key's original lyrics, written after the siege of Fort McHenry (top); the first published sheet music edition (bottom).

On the shore dimly seen through the mists of the deep,
Where the foe's haughty host in dread silence reposes,
What is that which the breeze, o'er the towering steep,
As it fitfully blows, half conceals, half discloses?
Now it catches the gleam of the morning's first beam,
In full glory reflected now shines in the stream:
'Tis the star-spangled banner, O long may it wave
O'er the land of the free and the home of the brave.

And where is that band who so vauntingly swore
That the havoc of war and the battle's confusion,
A home and a country, should leave us no more?
Their blood has washed out their foul footsteps' pollution.
No refuge could save the hireling and slave
From the terror of flight, or the gloom of the grave:
And the star-spangled banner in triumph doth wave,
O'er the land of the free and the home of the brave.

O thus be it ever, when freemen shall stand,
Between their lov'd home and the war's desolation.
Blest with vict'ry and peace, may the Heav'n rescued land,
Praise the Power that hath made and preserved us a nation!
Then conquer we must, when our cause it is just,
And this be our motto: "In God is our trust."
And the star-spangled banner in triumph shall wave,
O'er the land of the free and the home of the brave!

"The Star-Spangled Banner" is not easy to sing, but even its critics have long acknowledged its power. "It commences on a key so low that all may join in," Elias Nason wrote. "The melodic parts most naturally succeed each other, and, if I may so speak, are logically conjoined and bound together. It consists of solo, duet, and chorus, and thus in unity presents variety. It is bold, warlike, and majestic; stirring the profoundest emotions of the soul, and echoing through its deepest chambers something of the prospective grandeur of a mighty Nation tramping toward the loftiest heights of intellectual dominion."

THE STAR-SPANGLED BANNER

It may sound expected or even corny, but when I hear the national anthem I feel the honor—and the obligation—of being an American. "The Star-Spangled Banner" unites us as one nation. Written in a rush of inspiration by Francis Scott Key, the lyrics are visual and emotional. When we hear them, we're with him as he watches the bombs in the night and anxiously awaits the sight of the flag still intact. And, with him, we hope that our dreams for the republic will endure. The song leads us to think how far we've come, where we are, and how diligent we must be to continue moving forward.

"The Star-Spangled Banner" is an incredibly challenging song for any singer. Live, say at a major sporting event, you experience a delay from the stadium sound system that can put even the most focused singer in a difficult spot in terms of pitch. And then there is the melody, which covers about an octave and a half range—you need to be able to start low enough to finish those high notes at the end. But, like America, it's worth the trouble. —T.M.

The War of 1812 gave us, in the fullness of time, a national anthem, but that designation would not come for more than a century, when Congress elevated "The Star-Spangled Banner" to official status in 1931, in a law signed by President Herbert Hoover.

That Key's anthem focused on the flag rather than on the abstractions of Dickinson's "Liberty Song" or Hopkinson's "Hail Columbia" was telling, for the Stars and Stripes was becoming a more and more prevalent cultural emblem. First commissioned and designed during the Revolution, the flag was commonplace in the War of 1812. "The stars of the new flag represent the constellation of States rising in the West," a Continental Congressman wrote of the colors. "The idea was taken from the constellation Lyra; which, in the hand of Orpheus, signifies harmony. The stars were in a circle, symbolizing the perpetuity of the Union; the ring like the circling serpent of the Egyptians, signifying eternity. The thirteen stripes showed, together with the stars, the number of the United Colonies, and denoted the subordination of the States to the Union, as well as equality among themselves. The red color, which in the Roman day was the signal of defiance, denotes courage, the blue, fidelity, and the white, purity."

The War of 1812 was thus a milestone in the emergence of a sense of national identity.

Song spoke to the unifying impulses of the age. The themes of union and of America's special providential role in the world were part of the air of the time. When Jefferson and Adams died on the same day—the Fourth of July, 1826, the fiftieth anniversary of the Declaration of Independence—eulogists saw the coincidence as evidence, in the words of Daniel Webster, that as "their lives themselves were the gift of Providence," their deaths offered proof "that our country and its benefactors are objects of His care."

In 1831 the Reverend Samuel Francis Smith, then a student at Andover Theological Seminary in Massachusetts, wrote a hymn to the nation that spoke in Websterian terms about the American experiment. A twenty-four-year-old student, Smith had been reading over German patriotic hymns when he got the idea to compose one of his own. "Seizing a scrap of waste paper I began to write, and in half an hour, I think, the words stood upon it, substantially as they are sung today," Smith recalled. The tune for which he wrote was "God Save the King," the British national anthem popular since the mid-eighteenth century. "There is nothing more impudent in the history of plagiarism," the editor of the 1912 *Yale Book of American Verse* wrote, "than our appropriation of 'God Save the King' and dubbing it 'America.'"

The title of Smith's piece was simple but profound: "America," which became known as "My Country, 'Tis of Thee":

> My country! 'tis of thee,
> Sweet land of liberty,
> Of thee I sing:
> Land where my fathers died,
> Land of the pilgrims' pride,
> From every mountainside
> Let freedom ring!

> My native country, thee,
> Land of the noble free,
> Thy name I love;
> I love thy rocks and rills,
> Thy woods and templed hills;
> My heart with rapture thrills
> Like that above.

> Let music swell the breeze,
> And ring from all the trees
> Sweet freedom's song:

Let mortal tongues awake;
Let all that breathe partake;
Let rocks their silence break,
The sound prolong.

Our fathers' God! to Thee,
Author of liberty,
To Thee we sing.
Long may our land be bright
With freedom's holy light;
Protect us by Thy might,
Great God, our King!

A classmate of Smith's at Harvard College, Oliver Wendell Holmes, reflecting on his friend's poetic achievement, once wrote, "What is Fame? It is to write a hymn which sixty millions of people [the then population of the country] sing—that is fame." Holmes continued: "Now, there's Smith, his name will be honored by every school child in the land when I have been forgotten for a hundred years. He wrote 'My Country! 'Tis of Thee.' If he had said 'Our Country' the hymn would not have been immortal, but that 'My' was a master stroke. Everyone who sings the song at once feels a personal ownership in his native land. The hymn will last as long as the country."

The power of Smith's verses in part derives from what Bernice Johnson Reagon, a scholar of African American music and culture, curator emeritus at the Smithsonian Institution, and a distinguished professor emeritus at American University, called "the communal expression" of "'I,'" and from the diverse uses to which "My Country, 'Tis of Thee" has been put since its debut on the Fourth of July, 1831, at the Park Street Church in Boston. There were abolitionist versions like this one, published in 1839 under the pen name "Theta":

> My country, 'tis of thee,
> Stronghold of slavery—
> Of thee I sing:
> Land, where my fathers died,
> Where men *man*'s rights *deride;*
> From every mountainside,
> Thy deeds shall ring,
>
> My native country! Thee—
> Where all men are born free,
> If *white* their skin:
> I love thy hills and dales,
> Thy mounts and pleasant vales;
> But hate thy *negro* sales,
> As foulest sin.
>
> Let *wailing* swell the breeze,
> And ring from all the trees
> The *black* man's wrong;
> Let every tongue awake,
> Let *bond* and free partake.
> Let rocks their silence break,
> The sound prolong.
>
> Our father's God! To thee—
> Author of *Liberty*!

Samuel Francis Smith wrote "America," popularly known as "My Country, 'Tis of Thee," in 1831 as a seminary student in Andover, Massachusetts.

To thee we sing;
Soon may our land be bright,
With *holy Freedom*'s light,
Protect us by thy might,
Great God, our King.

At the Union's Camp Saxton, in South Carolina, Smith's hymn was the first thing sung by some freed slaves when emancipation came, as 1862 turned into 1863. It was the last thing sung, C. A. Browne noted, by dying men among Colonel Theodore Roosevelt's Rough Riders in Cuba during the Spanish-American War, thus becoming the final words of men fighting for an imperialist vision of Anglo-Saxon civilization. And it gave Martin Luther King, Jr., his peroration at the March on Washington in August 1963.

MY COUNTRY, 'TIS OF THEE

When you hear it played simply—on a piano, for instance—it feels like a hymn, something I might've sung in church as a boy. With an orchestra, it becomes regal and majestic, a song worthy of presidential inaugurations. We see this throughout so much early music—composers using familiar melodies and rewriting the lyrics for their current political or cultural climate. We still do it. We do it because it works. Listeners, almost unknowingly, recognize an emotion from the past while clinging to the modern message. (In our own time, think about how Kanye West played off a line from Ray Charles's "I Got a Woman" in his "Gold Digger" single.)

John Dickinson did this with "The Liberty Song," but Samuel Francis Smith took things to an even higher level by appropriating "God Save the King" for American hearts and voices. I say "hearts" because "My Country, 'Tis of

> Thee" was—*is*—really about putting not a monarch but the nation itself, and the ideas on which it's founded and with which it endures, at the center of our imaginative lives.
>
> What we say as a people—and what we sing as a people—matters, for even if we fall short of the ideal, we've got to keep that ideal in front of us, like a beacon through the darkness. "My Country, 'Tis of Thee" is one of those beacons.   —T.M.

Whites and Blacks, men and women, enslaved and free, the powerful and the powerless: "My Country, 'Tis of Thee" was sung by sundry voices for sundry reasons, in calm and in storm. In a way, Oliver Wendell Holmes may have been more right than even he knew when he praised Smith for giving Americans the means to sing not only of *the* country—the task of Dickinson, Hopkinson, and Key—but of one's *own* country, one's own understanding of what the nation, so flawed and yet so noble, so incomplete yet so full of promise, had been, was, and, most important, could be.

That, at least, was the aspiration. The idea of liberty was animating, but it was limited. An English visitor to America in the Age of Jackson, Frances Trollope, was blunt about the inconsistencies of democracy in the United States. "You will see them with one hand hoisting the cap of liberty, and with the other flogging their slaves," Mrs. Trollope, the mother of the novelist Anthony Trollope, wrote in her 1832 book *Domestic Manners of the Americans.* "You will see them one hour lecturing their mob on the indefeasible rights of man, and the next driving from their homes the children of the soil, whom they have bound themselves to protect by the most solemn of treaties."

Her harsh words about the treatment of Native Americans—those whom she called "the children of the soil"—were more than justified. For generations, white Americans had taken the land they wanted to take, driving the native inhabitants ever westward, forever displacing them at will despite treaties and promises. The story is tragic, depressing, and irredeemable. From New England, Jeremiah Evarts attempted to mount a moral case against the removal policies of the first several decades of the nineteenth century, but to no lasting avail. "The questions have forced themselves upon us, as a nation—*What is to become of the Indians? Have they any rights? If they have, What are these rights? And how are they to be secured?*" Evarts wrote in the first of his essays in a series entitled "Present Crisis in the Condition of the American Indians," published in 1829.

Harriet Beecher Stowe's sister, Catharine Beecher, also joined the fight, writing a "Circular Addressed to the Benevolent Ladies of the U. States" in December 1829. Lamenting that "it has become almost a certainty that these people are to have their lands torn from them, and to be driven into western wilds and to final annihilation," Stowe wrote that only "the feelings of a humane and Christian nation" could "prevent the unhallowed sacrifice" of removal.

Nothing, however, would carry the day against the will of the white powers. "I was a stranger in a strange land," John Rollin Ridge, a child of the Cherokee Nation that was driven to the Trail of Tears, wrote from California. Such was the fate of the Native Americans, and the music of the tribes spoke of gods and of men, of creation and of loss, of joy and of danger.

One song of the Choctaw that dates from at least the 1830s—years in which the tribe was removed from Mississippi to Oklahoma—is entitled "Long Sought Home" and can be translated this way:

> Someday when I die
> The Great Spirit above will hold me.
>
> Because of the Creator when I die
> I am going to be in a good land.

Because of the Creator's mercy
I will be there,
In that distant heavenly land.

The Navajo sing a "Song of the Earth":

The Earth is beautiful.
The Earth is beautiful.
The Earth is beautiful.

Below the East, the Earth, its face toward the East.
The top of its head is beautiful.
The soles of its feet are beautiful.
Its feet, they are beautiful.

"Someday when I die / The Great Spirit above will hold me," the Choctaw sang on the Trail of Tears—the forcible removal of Native Americans from their ancestral lands.

Its legs, they are beautiful.

Its body, it is beautiful.

Its chest, its breast, its head feather,

they are beautiful. . . .

In his landmark survey of America's music, Richard Crawford cited an 1822 article by Lewis Cass, governor of the Michigan Territory, who quoted a Miami Native American lyric, "I will go and get my friends—I will go and get my friends—I am anxious to see my enemies. A clear sky is my friend, and it is him I am seeking."

Cass explained that the song was designed to inspire action. "The manner in which these words are sung cannot be described to the reader," he wrote. "There is a strong expiration of breath at the commencement of each sentence, and a sudden elevation of the voice at the termination. The Chief, as he passes, looks every person sternly in the face. Those who are disposed to join the expedition exclaim *Yeh, Yeh, Yeh*, with a powerful tone of voice; and this exclamation is continually repeated during the whole ceremony. It is, if I may so speak, the evidence of their enlistment. Those who are silent decline the invitation."

To Crawford, "Cass's account squares with what are now understood as timeless Native American practices. One of the song's traits . . . is that its music has a specific purpose: in this case to recruit volunteers for a mission of war. The text's brevity does not mean that the performance was short. Many commentators of the time reported Native Americans' tendency to repeat bits of text and music incessantly, and noted the long stretches of time that performances could fill."

The Ojibwa George Copway was an important writer of Native descent, publishing *The Life, History, and Travels of Kah-ge-ga-gah-bowh* in 1847. In it he shared a "dream song" that he said had come to him at age twelve:

It is I who travel in the winds,
It is I who whisper in the breeze,
I shake the trees,
I shake the earth,
I trouble the waters on every land.

"My son," Copway's father told him, "*the god of the winds* is kind to you; the aged tree, I hope, may indicate long life; the wind may indicate that you will travel much; the water which you saw, and the winds, will carry your canoe safely through the waves." It was, in a sense, a father's prayer for a son who would always be in a strange country.

Samuel Smith had drafted "My Country, 'Tis of Thee" in his quarters in Andover in February 1831; a month before, on New Year's Day, twenty-five miles away in Boston, the abolitionist William Lloyd Garrison began publishing his newspaper, the *Liberator.* "Assenting to the 'self-evident truth' maintained in the American Declaration of Independence, 'that all men are created equal, and endowed by their Creator with certain inalienable rights—among which are life, liberty, and the pursuit of happiness,'" Garrison wrote in the inaugural issue, "I shall strenuously contend for the immediate enfranchisement of our slave population."

Two years earlier, in 1829, David Walker,

Founded in 1831—the same year Samuel Francis Smith wrote "My Country, 'Tis of Thee"—William Lloyd Garrison's *Liberator* led the abolitionist cause.

whose father was enslaved, had published his *Appeal to the Colored Citizens of the World,* a pamphlet that worried Southern slaveholders and inspired antislavery advocates. The Black people of the United States, Walker wrote, were "the most degraded, wretched, and abject set of beings that ever lived since the world began, and I pray God that none like us ever may live again until time shall be no more."

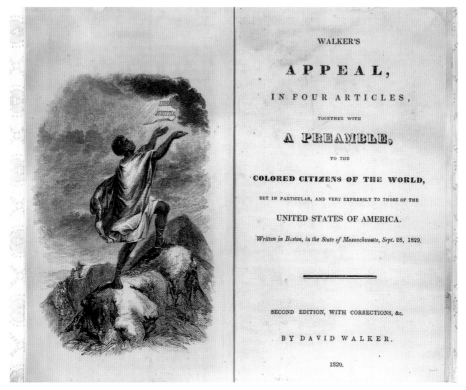

David Walker's *Appeal,* published in 1829, closed with a hymn drawn from Psalm 10 that called on the Lord to "Defend the poor from harm."

Looking back on the Age of Jackson and of Walker's *Appeal,* W. E. B. Du Bois—author, activist, and one of the founders of the civil rights organization National Association for the Advancement of Colored People (NAACP)—recalled that there had been a passing interest in "The Sorrow Songs" of the African American milieu. "Away back in the thirties"—the 1830s—"the melody of these slave songs stirred the nation," Du Bois recalled, "but the songs were soon half forgotten." Such voices, however, could not be forever stilled. Writing in his 1903 book, *The Souls of Black Folk,* Du Bois excerpted an old spiritual:

> I walk through the churchyard
> To lay this body down;
> I know moon-rise, I know star-rise;
> I walk in the moonlight, I walk in the starlight;
> I'll lie in the grave and stretch out my arms,
> I'll go to judgment in the evening of the day,
> And my soul and thy soul shall meet that day,
> When I lay this body down.

The origins and development of music among African Americans make a saga unto themselves, a story of breathtaking creativity and genius flowering amid the most inhumane of circumstances. Drawing on African and Caribbean traditions, inventing their own, and producing a body of work that would ultimately find expression in genres that included gospel, jazz, blues, and, centuries on, hip-hop, Black Americans forged a remarkable cultural life and legacy that reaches far beyond any arbitrary racial category. "They that walked in darkness sang songs in the olden days—Sorrow Songs—for they were weary at heart . . . ," Du Bois wrote. "And so by fateful chance the Negro folk-song—the rhythmic cry of the slave—stands today not simply as the sole American music, but as the most beautiful expression of human experience born this side the seas."

The journey had begun, like so much else, with life in slavery. "I have often been utterly astonished, since I came to the north, to find persons who could speak of the singing, among slaves, as evidence of their contentment and happiness," Frederick Douglass wrote in his 1845 *Narrative of the Life of Frederick Douglass, An American Slave.* "It is impossible to conceive of a greater mistake. Slaves sing most when they are most unhappy. The songs of the slave represent the sorrows of his heart; and he is relieved by them, only as an aching heart is relieved by its tears. To Douglass, the songs of the enslaved embodied the tragedy of human chattel.

There were songs like "Sold Off to Georgy [Georgia]":

> Farewell, fellow servants! O-ho! O-ho!
> I'm going way to leave you; O-ho! O-ho!
> I'm going to leave the old county, O-ho! O-ho!
> I'm sold off to Georgy, O-ho, O-ho!

The same theme informed another song, about being sold and shipped in chains:

> See these poor souls from Africa
> Transported to America:
> We are stolen and sold to Georgia, will you go along with me?
> We are stolen and sold to Georgia, go sound the jubilee.
>
> See wives and husbands sold apart,
> The children's screams!—it breaks my heart. . . .
>
> O gracious Lord! When shall it be
> That we poor souls shall all be free? . . .
> Lord, break them Slavery powers—will you go along with me?
> Lord, break them Slavery powers, go sound the jubilee.

Dear Lord! Dear Lord! When Slavery'll cease,
Then we poor souls can have our peace;
There's a better day a-coming, will you go along with me?
There's a better day a-coming, go sound the jubilee.

The expectation of that better day informed much of the music of the enslaved. As Douglass plotted his escape from bondage in eastern Maryland, he and his compatriots, he recalled, sometimes let their hopes get the better of their judgment. Reflecting on the master from whom he broke away, Douglass wrote, "I am the more inclined to think that he suspected us, because, prudent as we were, as I now look back, I can see that we did many silly things, very well calculated to awaken suspicion," continuing:

> We were, at times, remarkably buoyant, singing hymns and making joyous exclamations, almost as triumphant in their tone as if we had reached a land of freedom and safety. A keen observer might have detected in our repeated singing of
>
> > "O Canaan, sweet Canaan,
> > I am bound for the land of Canaan,"
>
> something more than a hope of reaching heaven. We meant to reach the *north*—and the north was our Canaan.
>
> > "I thought I heard them say,
> > There were lions in the way,
> > I don't expect to stay
> > Much longer here.
> > Run to Jesus—shun the danger—
> > I don't expect to stay
> > Much longer here."

It was, Douglass wrote, "a favorite air, and had a double meaning. In the lips of some, it meant the expectation of a speedy summons to the world of spirits; but, in the lips of our company, it simply meant a speedy pilgrimage toward a free state, and deliverance from all the evils and dangers of slavery."

The "double meaning" of which Douglass wrote is also called "masking"—the tradition in African American music of apparently singing about one thing while in fact singing about another. To sing of deliverance from sin, for instance, was also to sing of deliverance from slavery and from discrimination without provoking a white backlash. "Swing Low, Sweet Chariot" is a classic example; the chariot isn't just about going to a heaven beyond the skies, but to a freedom beyond the Mason-Dixon Line.

As a conductor on the loose network of escape routes that would come to be known as the Underground Railroad, Harriet Tubman used song as a signal as she led the enslaved north toward freedom through terrifying darkness in the middle years of the nineteenth century. Born circa 1820 into bondage in Maryland, Tubman escaped to Philadelphia in 1849. The story is told that Tubman sang these words as she prepared to flee:

When that old chariot comes,
I'm going to leave you,
I'm bound for the promised land,
Friends, I'm going to leave you.

I'm sorry, friends, to leave you,
Farewell! Oh, farewell!
But I'll meet you in the morning,
Farewell! Oh, farewell!

I'll meet you in the morning,
When you reach the promised land;
On the other side of Jordan,
For I'm bound for the promised land.

It was the most daunting of missions, but Tubman was determined. "For I had reasoned this out in my mind: there were one of two things I had a right to, liberty, or death," she recalled, and "if I could not have one, I would have the other; for no man should take me alive. I should fight for my liberty as long as my strength lasted, and when the time came for me to go, the Lord would let them take me."

On the plantation from which she fled, her "farewell song was long remembered in the cabins." When she crossed into safe territory in the North, she recalled, "I looked at my hands to see I was the same person now [that] I was free. There was such a glory over everything, the sun came like gold through the trees, and over the fields, and I felt like I was in Heaven."

To her credit, her mind was never far from those who remained in the hell

Harriet Tubman sang spirituals as signals to the enslaved along what came to be known as the Underground Railroad.

of enslavement, and she devoted herself to making freedom possible for others under the most dangerous of conditions. "At one time the pursuit was very close and vigorous," Sarah H. Bradford wrote in *Harriet Tubman: The Moses of Her People,* which was based on interviews with Tubman. Slave-catchers were out in force. "The woods were scoured in all directions, every house was visited, and every person stopped and questioned as to a band of black fugitives, known to be fleeing through that part of the country. Harriet had a large party with her then; the children were sleeping the sound sleep that opium gives; but all the others were on the alert, each one hidden behind his own tree, and silent as death." Tubman left them to secure food, slipping off for a time.

Bradford then recounted the evening from the perspective of the huddled slaves: "How long she is away! Has she been caught and carried off, and if so what is to become of them? Hark! There is a sound of singing in the distance, coming nearer and nearer. And these are the words of the unseen singer . . ."

> Hail, oh hail, ye happy spirits,
> Death no more shall make you fear,
> Grief nor sorrow, pain nor anguish,
> Shall no more distress you there.
>
> Around Him are ten thousand angels,
> Always ready to obey command;
> They are always hovering round you,
> Till you reach the heavenly land.
>
> Jesus, Jesus will go with you,
> He will lead you to his throne;
> He who died, has gone before you,
> Through the wine-press all alone.
>
> He whose thunders shake creation,
> He who bids the planets roll;

He who rides upon the tempest,
And whose scepter sways the whole.

Dark and thorny is the pathway,
Where the pilgrim makes his ways;
But beyond this vale of sorrow,
Lie the fields of endless days.

Tubman sometimes sang another song as well, one drawn from the story of Exodus, the most familiar of images to a people for whom churches, religious gatherings, and spirituals were crucial:

Oh go down, Moses,
Way down into Egypt's land;
Tell old Pharaoh
Let my people go.

Oh Pharaoh said he would go cross,
Let my people go,
And don't get lost in the wilderness,
Let my people go.

Oh go down, Moses,
Way down into Egypt's land;
Tell old Pharaoh
Let my people go.

You may hinder me here, but you can't up there,
Let my people go,
He sits in . . . Heaven and answers prayer,
Let my people go!

Oh go down, Moses,
Way down into Egypt's land,
Tell old Pharaoh,
Let my people go.

Sometimes there would be a call-and-response between conductor and passenger. Tubman would sing:

When that old chariot comes,
Who's going with me?

And the reply would come:

When that old chariot comes,
I'm going with you. . . .

Once in freedom, Tubman recalled, now-former slaves would raise their
voices in thanksgiving:

Glory to God and Jesus, too,
One more soul got safe;
Oh, go and carry the news,
One more soul got safe. . . .

Glory to God in the highest,
Glory to God and Jesus, too,
For all these souls now safe.

*   *   *

One close Tubman ally, Senator William H. Seward of New York, had long articulated a vision of an emancipated America. In opposing the Compromise of 1850—including the Fugitive Slave Act, which required the return of the enslaved to their owners—Seward had said that he foresaw "countless generations . . . rising up and passing in dim and shadowy review before us; and a voice comes forth from their serried ranks, saying: 'Waste your treasures and your armies, if you will; raze your fortifications to the ground; sink your navies into the sea; transmit to us even a dishonored name, if you must; but the soil you hold in trust for us— give it to us free.'"

The Founders and their heirs had sought to live, as Lincoln put it in Springfield in 1858, "half slave and half free." Prevailing racist views of identity and power made this hypocrisy possible and durable, and evolving understandings of equality and liberty led to what Seward would call "the irrepressible conflict"— a war to settle, at last, whether slavery could coexist with American democracy.

CHAPTER THREE

MINE EYES HAVE SEEN THE GLORY

Sing it again!
> —ABRAHAM LINCOLN, on hearing "The Battle Hymn of the Republic"

The year of jubilee is come . . . !
> —From "Blow Ye the Trumpet, Blow!," a favorite hymn of Frederick Douglass

Frederick Douglass was going home. With the successful publication of his *Narrative* in 1845, Douglass had left America for Great Britain to tour and lecture for twenty-one months. In 1847, as he prepared to return to the United States, the abolitionist Julia Griffiths and her brother, T. Powis Griffiths, composed a piece called "Farewell Song of Frederick Douglass: On Quitting England for America—the Land of his Birth." Playing off the promise, though not the reality, of the country evoked by Key's "Star-Spangled Banner," the Griffithses depicted Britain as the true land of liberty, writing:

> Farewell to the land of the free! Farewell to the land of the brave.
> Alas! That my country should be America! Land of the slave . . .

The Griffithses had captured a great tragic contradiction at the heart of the American experiment: that a nation conceived in liberty preserved and

Song was an essential element in inspiring Frederick Douglass to plan and execute his escape from slavery.

perpetuated human slavery. "How is it," the eighteenth-century English man of letters Samuel Johnson had wondered, "that we hear the loudest yelps for liberty among the drivers of the negroes?"

How, indeed? Few spoke of slavery in America more incisively and eloquently than Douglass, who, on returning to the United States at midcentury, engaged in what the Griffithses had described, in the "Farewell Song," as a war against evil:

> Shall I, like a coward, not join the fight?
> Shrink from the onslaught when battle is raging
> Scared by the enemy's tyrannous might?

The answer was an emphatic *no.* In an Independence Day oration at Rochester, New York, delivered on the fifth of July in 1852, Douglass offered a nuanced yet passionate view of the meaning of America.

> Fellow-citizens, pardon me, allow me to ask, why am I called upon to speak here today? What have I, or those I represent, to do with your national independence? Are the great principles of political freedom and of natural justice, embodied in that Declaration of Independence, extended to us? . . .
>
> I am not included within the pale of this glorious anniversary! Your high independence only reveals the immeasurable distance between us. The blessings in which you, this day, rejoice, are not enjoyed in common.—The rich inheritance of justice, liberty, prosperity and independence, bequeathed by your fathers, is shared by you, not by me. The sunlight that brought life and healing to you, has brought stripes and death to me. This Fourth of July is *yours,* not *mine. You* may rejoice, *I* must mourn.

Douglass was part of a chorus of voices seeking to end slavery, but there were also voices rising to defend enslavement. In March 1861, Alexander H. Stephens, the vice president of the newly formed Confederate States of America, spoke about the white Southern cause in an address at Savannah, Georgia.

"The new [Confederate] constitution has put at rest, forever, all the agitating questions relating to our peculiar institution, African slavery, as it exists amongst us [and] the proper status of the negro in our form of civilization," Stephens said. "This was the immediate cause of the late rupture and present revolution."

Stephens linked the Confederate view of perpetual racial inequality to great scientific insights, suggesting that Black inferiority was a principle as well established as the orbit of the earth around the sun or the circulation of blood in the human body. "With us," he said of the newly seceded government, "all of the white race, however high or low, rich or poor, are equal in the eye of the law. Not so with the negro. Subordination is his place. He, by nature, or by the curse against Canaan, is fitted for that condition which he occupies in our system," adding: "I cannot permit myself to doubt the ultimate success of a full recognition of this principle throughout the civilized and enlightened world." It might take time, he acknowledged, but he claimed to be confident of eventual victory.

There, then, were two starkly divergent views of humankind that fed the flames of what Lincoln called the "fiery trial" of the Civil War. We know that Douglass was right and Stephens was wrong, but the adjudication of the argument would claim three-quarters of a million lives and very nearly end the American Union. A question raised by the Griffithses' "Farewell Song" for Douglass required a definitive answer—would America remain the "land of the slave," or could it, in Francis Scott Key's language, genuinely become the "land of the free"? And so two songs, written three and a half decades and an ocean apart, framed a conundrum that only combat would resolve.

The prose of the war could be splendid and often had its own quasi-musical rhythms. Like Douglass's, Abraham Lincoln's words echo through the ages. Consider the president's Second Annual Message to Congress, in late 1862:

> Fellow-citizens, *we* cannot escape history. We of this Congress and this administration, will be remembered in spite of ourselves. No personal significance, or insignificance, can spare one or another of us. The fiery trial through which we pass, will light us down, in honor or dishonor, to the latest generation. We *say* we are for the Union. The world will not forget that we say this. We know how to save the Union. The world knows we do know how to save it. We—even *we here*—hold the power and bear the responsibility. In *giving* freedom to the *slave,* we *assure* freedom to the *free*—honorable alike in what we give, and what we preserve. We shall nobly save, or meanly lose, the last best hope of earth.

Prose doesn't get much better than that, yet song was as much a part of Civil War America as speech.

From Chicago, George F. Root composed perhaps the earliest song of the war after Fort Sumter, "The First Gun Is Fired," which he had ready within three days of the Confederate attack on the federal installation in Charleston Harbor:

> The first gun is fired!
> "May God protect the right!"
> Let the freeborn sons of the North arise
> In power's avenging might;
> Shall the glorious Union our fathers have made,
> By ruthless hands be sunder'd?

And we of freedom's sacred rights
By trait'rous foes be plunder'd?
Arise! arise! arise!
And gird ye for the fight!
And let our watchword ever be,
"May God protect the right!"

He later put Henry S. Washburn's poem "The Vacant Chair," about a family's grief at the death of a soldier, to music:

We shall meet but we shall miss him,
There will be one vacant chair;
We shall linger to caress him,
While we breathe our evening prayer. . . .

True, they tell us wreaths of glory
Evermore will deck his brow,
But this soothes the anguish only,
Sweeping o'er our heartstrings now.
Sleep today, O early fallen,
In thy green and narrow bed.
Dirges from the pine and cypress
Mingle with the tears we shed.

The music of the Union cause—"John Brown's Body," "The Battle Hymn of the Republic," "The Battle Cry of Freedom," "We Are Coming, Father Abraham," "Marching Through Georgia," and the songs of the enslaved—was to fill the air, and to fire the imagination, with images of righteous struggle. The Hutchinson Family Singers, who hailed from New Hampshire, had prepared the ground in the antebellum years, singing songs about emancipation and liberty to broad audiences. During the war, the Hutchinsons put John Greenleaf Whittier's abolitionist poem "We Wait beneath the Furnace Blast" to music:

> What breaks the oath
> Of the men o' the South?
> What whets the knife
> For the Union's life?—
> Hark to the answer: *Slavery!*

To listen to the music of the Union cause, there could be no higher calling, no more divine mission, than the abolition of slavery and the salvation of the constitutional order conceived at Philadelphia in 1787. In "The Battle Cry of Freedom," Root wrote:

> The Union forever, Hurrah, boys, hurrah!
> Down with the traitor, Up with the star;
> While we rally round the flag, boys, rally once again,
> Shouting the battle cry of freedom . . .
>
> We will welcome to our numbers the loyal, true and brave,
> Shouting the battle cry of freedom,
> And although they may be poor, not a man shall be a slave,
> Shouting the battle cry of freedom.
>
> So we're springing to the call from the East and from the West,
> Shouting the battle cry of freedom,
> And we'll hurl the rebel crew from the land we love the best,
> Shouting the battle cry of freedom.

In the fullness of time, Lincoln would purportedly tell Root that the composer had "done more than a hundred generals and a thousand orators" by framing the conflict so powerfully. Music, however, could mask some of the war's complexities. Lincoln's history, and America's, would be nobler if he had always been a fearless soldier in the cause of abolition.

But he was not. In his anguish over slavery and Union, Lincoln was in some senses a representative white American—a man whose journey to a more perfect Union was complicated by the prevailing white prejudices and economic realities of the time. "I am naturally anti-slavery," Lincoln wrote in April 1864. "If slavery is not wrong, nothing is wrong. I cannot remember when I did not so think, and feel." As early as 1854, speaking in Peoria, Illinois, Lincoln had called slavery a "monstrous injustice," saying: "Let us re-adopt the Declaration of Independence, and with it, the practices, and policy, which harmonize with it. . . . If we do this, we shall not only have saved the Union; but we shall have so saved it, as to make, and to keep it, forever worthy of the saving."

He was less certain, though, about exactly how to design and implement this plan of salvation.

His consuming concern on coming to the presidency was the rescue of the Union so long as slavery remained an exclusively Southern institution. In 1858, Lincoln had said, "I will say then that I am not, nor ever have been, in favor of bringing about in any way the social and political equality of the white and black races." At his first inauguration, in 1861, Lincoln tried to allay slaveholders' anxieties, saying, "Apprehension seems to exist among the people of the Southern States that by the accession of a Republican Administration their property and their peace and personal security are to be endangered. There has never been any reasonable cause for such apprehension. Indeed, the most ample evidence to the contrary has all the while existed and been open to their inspection. It is found in nearly all the published speeches of him who now addresses you. I do but quote from one of those speeches when I declare that—'I have no purpose, directly or indirectly, to interfere with the institution of slavery in the States where it exists. I believe I have no lawful right to do so, and I have no inclination to do so.'"

By the summer of 1862, however, it had become evident to him that emancipation, even in a limited way, would be militarily wise while having the virtue

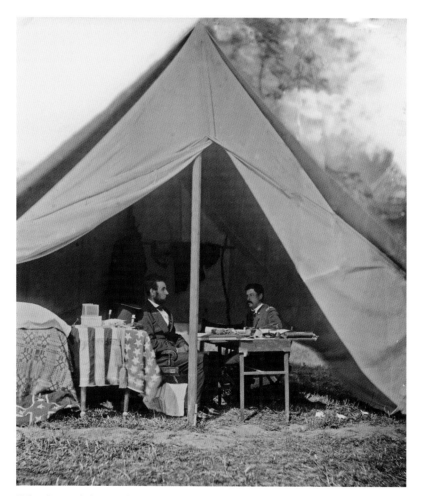

"The fiery trial": President Lincoln in conference with General George B. McClellan at Antietam. The Union victory there helped convince the president to issue the Emancipation Proclamation.

of being morally right. After the Confederate defeat at Antietam in September, Lincoln told his cabinet that he had struck a bargain with God: If the Union forces could prevail in Maryland, he, the president, would move on emancipation. Now that that victory had come, Lincoln said, he was ready to act—and with the Emancipation Proclamations of September 1862 and New Year's Day 1863, he imbued the Union cause with ultimate moral meaning.

Music greeted the order that the enslaved in states in rebellion would be "forever free." As Eileen Southern, the historian of African American music, wrote, "Black men assembled in 'rejoicing meetings' all over the land on the last night of December in 1862, waiting for the stroke of midnight to bring freedom to those slaves in the secessionist states." In Washington, a gathering of African Americans sang Harriet Tubman's old favorite:

"Forever free": The text of Lincoln's Emancipation Proclamation, which liberated the enslaved in the states in rebellion against the United States of America.

> Go down, Moses,
> Way down in Egypt land;
> Tell old Pharaoh,
> Let my people go.

According to Southern, a woman in the crowd offered a new verse, to the delight of what was described as "the vast assembly":

Go down, Abraham,

Away down in Dixie's land;

Tell Jeff Davis

To let my people go.

GO DOWN, MOSES and SWING LOW, SWEET CHARIOT

Haunting and compelling, "Go Down, Moses" moves me deeply. I am pulled into the struggle for freedom with the minor chords and the major sentiment of this spiritual tune. Whatever your ethnicity, whatever your background, you can feel the African rhythm down in your soul. As a well-known African American spiritual, it lends itself to great artistic interpretation. (One of the most popular is by the incomparable Louis Armstrong, whose distinct voice could take any song to a new place.)

"Swing Low, Sweet Chariot" is another favorite spiritual of mine. Joan Baez sang this at the Woodstock festival. There's power in the intersection of spiritual and folk music. And it's great—and very American—that one of the most famous songs of all time was written by an Oklahoma enslaved person, Wallace Willis. I envision that moment when the unimaginable demands of his life in enslavement were overwhelming and he felt this deep-down longing for freedom—then realized that the only freedom he might know lay in death.

—T.M.

Lincoln's decision on emancipation came in the same months that Julia Ward Howe's "The Battle Hymn of the Republic" was becoming popular. A poet and activist from Boston, Howe had joined her husband and a few others in coming south to watch the Grand Review of the Army of the Potomac at Bailey's Crossroads in northern Virginia. Inspired by what she'd seen, Howe rose in the night in her room at Willard's City Hotel near the White House and, in the gloom, wrote new verses to a familiar piece. The tune for which she was composing was well known in abolitionist circles and among Union soldiers as "John Brown's Body," an anthem commemorating the antislavery martyr who had been executed after leading a raid on Harpers Ferry:

> John Brown's body lies a-mouldering in the grave,
> John Brown's body lies a-mouldering in the grave,
> John Brown's body lies a-mouldering in the grave,
> But his soul goes marching on.
>
> Glory, glory, hallelujah,
> Glory, glory, hallelujah,
> Glory, glory, hallelujah,
> His soul goes marching on.
>
> He's gone to be a soldier in the Army of the Lord,
> He's gone to be a soldier in the Army of the Lord,
> He's gone to be a soldier in the Army of the Lord,
> His soul goes marching on. . . .
>
> John Brown died that the slaves might be free,
> John Brown died that the slaves might be free,
> John Brown died that the slaves might be free,
> His soul goes marching on.

The immediate occasion for Howe's own verses came from her own singing of "John Brown's Body" with the soldiers she had encountered earlier that day. One of her party, the Reverend James Freeman Clarke, had challenged her to improve on the existing song. "Mrs. Howe, why do you not write some good words for that stirring tune?" Howe rose to the challenge. "And so, to pacify the dear old man, I promised to try."

The poem she scribbled in the darkness elevated the fight for the Union to the noblest of planes:

> Mine eyes have seen the glory of the coming of the Lord:
> He is trampling out the vintage where the grapes of wrath are
>   stored;
> He hath loosed the fateful lightning of His terrible swift sword:
> His truth is marching on.

> I have seen Him in the watch fires of a hundred circling camps,
> They have builded Him an altar in the evening dews and damps;
> I can read His righteous sentence by the dim and flaring lamps:
> His day is marching on.

> I have read a fiery gospel writ in burnished rows of steel:
> "As ye deal with My contemners, so with you My grace shall deal;
> Let the Hero, born of woman, crush the serpent with his heel,
> Since God is marching on."

> He has sounded forth the trumpet that shall never call retreat;

In 1861, Julia Ward Howe awoke in the night at Willard's City Hotel in Washington, D.C., to scribble down the verses to what became "The Battle Hymn of the Republic."

He is sifting out the hearts of men before His judgment-seat:
Oh, be swift, my soul, to answer Him! Be jubilant, my feet!
Our God is marching on.

In the beauty of the lilies Christ was born across the sea,
With a glory in his bosom that transfigures you and me:
As he died to make men holy, let us die to make men free,
While God is marching on.

The vision of the armies of the Lord on the march in the cause of true justice was compelling, and the verses were first published in the *Atlantic Monthly* in February 1862. "Do you want this, and do you like it, and have you any room for

it in the January number?" Howe had written *Atlantic* editor James Fields, who paid her five dollars for the poem, which he printed on the cover of the magazine with a title of his devising: "The Battle Hymn of the Republic" was fully born.

Lincoln loved it, calling out, "Sing it again!" after hearing Charles McCabe, a Methodist minister and a chaplain in the 122nd Ohio Volunteer Infantry, perform it in the hall of the House of Representatives on Tuesday, February 2, 1864. "Take it all in all," Lincoln later told McCabe, "the song and the singing, that was the best I ever heard."

By mid-1862 the Union needed more soldiers willing, as Howe had put it, to "die to make men free." President Lincoln called for

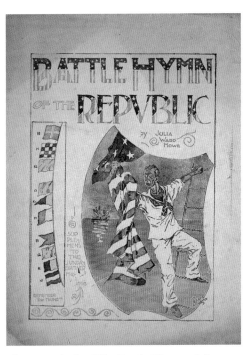

Sheet music for "The Battle Hymn of the Republic," the title *Atlantic Monthly* editor James Fields gave to Howe's poem.

three hundred thousand additional soldiers, inspiring this Biblical poem from a Quaker, James Sloan Gibbons, which was first published in the New York *Evening Post* of Wednesday, July 16, 1862, and set to music:

> We are coming, Father Abraham, three hundred thousand more,
> From Mississippi's winding stream and from New England's shore.
> We leave our plows and workshops, our wives and children dear,
> With hearts too full for utterance, with but a silent tear.
> We dare not look behind us but steadfastly before.
> We are coming, Father Abraham, three hundred thousand more!
> We are coming, coming, our Union to restore,
> We are coming, Father Abraham, three hundred thousand more!

THE BATTLE HYMN OF THE REPUBLIC, THE BATTLE CRY OF FREEDOM, and WE ARE COMING, FATHER ABRAHAM

"The Battle Hymn" is one of my first musical memories. As a young child, I went to audition for a part in a play. Instead of giving me a song to sing, they asked if I knew anything, and I knew Julia Ward Howe's majestic song (or at least the first verse). A big part of its power is how it links the human and the divine, the small and the large, the particular and the universal. Told from the perspective of a soldier for justice—and it could be a traditional soldier under arms or anyone who fights to right wrongs—"The Battle Hymn" is about pilgrims on earth taking on the Lord's work. This can be tricky—humility means we can't confuse our will with God's—but history tells us that we make our greatest advances in America when religious conviction informs political action. From abolition to civil rights, ministers of the Lord have led us to higher ground.

In "The Battle Cry of Freedom" we have a great example of music's incredible ability to unify words, beat, and melody into a form that can motivate us in times of war and struggle. I can picture Union soldiers marching off with a righteous cause in their heart and this drumbeat driving them onward.

With "Father Abraham," I'm struck by the first line: "We are coming, Father Abraham, three hundred thousand more." That's a lot of lives unified and willing to die for the Union cause. I love that this song feels like an upbeat march musically, even though lyrically it's clear that these troops left their families for bloody rivers and death alongside their brothers. But you can hear the belief in their cause in the upbeat tempo. It's a song for the beginning of a war, when spirits and righteousness are high.   —T.M.

America's music could be as racially complicated as the country itself, a fact well illustrated by the man known as "America's Troubadour," Stephen C. Foster. Widely considered the most successful songwriter of the mid-nineteenth century, he wrote for the blackface minstrel stage, a popular genre in the middle decades of the 1800s. "Essentially it consisted of an exploitation of the slave's style of music and dancing by white men, who blackened their faces with burnt cork and went on the stage to sing 'Negro songs' (also called 'Ethiopian songs'), to perform dances derived from those of the slaves, and to tell jokes based on slave life," Eileen Southern wrote. Two archetypes drove the shows: the enslaved plantation hand "Jim Crow" and the enslaved urban "dandy dressed in the latest fashion, who boasted of his exploits among the ladies," known as "Zip Coon."

Foster, who drank himself to death in 1864, at age thirty-seven, was famous for "Old Uncle Ned," "Oh! Susanna," "My Old Kentucky Home," and "Old Folks at Home" ("Swanee River"), among others. During the war he wrote a few conventional songs that drew on the emotions of the time. One was 1862's "Was My Brother in the Battle?":

> Tell me, tell me, weary soldier From the rude and stirring wars,
> Was my brother in the battle where you gained those noble scars?
> He was ever brave and valiant, and I know he never fled.
> Was his name among the wounded or numbered with the dead?
> Was my brother in the battle when the tide of war ran high?
> You would know him in a thousand by his dark and flashing eye.
>
> Tell me, tell me weary soldier, will he never come again,
> Did he suffer 'mid the wounded or die among the slain?

WAS MY BROTHER IN THE BATTLE?

Stephen Foster is acknowledged by many as the first professional songwriter—certainly one of the first songwriters in the sense of how we think of songwriters today. Who doesn't know "Oh! Susanna"? His ability to find a melody and lyric that touched the American public was unmatched. "Was My Brother in the Battle?" is so incredibly sad—sung from the point of view of a sibling who's wondering what has become of his brother in harm's way.

Strikingly, this timeless question of war is never answered. We are left to wonder and share in Foster's words of belief—whatever the brother's fate, "He was ever brave and valiant." Foster knew that there was incredible power in leaving the question unresolved, for the song leaves us longing to know, and engaged long after the music stops. —T.M.

A year later, in 1863, Foster published "For the Dear Old Flag I Die!" with lyrics by George Cooper. Like "Was My Brother in the Battle?" it was a meditation on the tragedy of war. As "Death's cold hand" grips the "wounded drummer boy," the lad finds comfort in thoughts of his mother, and of home:

> For the dear old Flag I die,
> Said the wounded drummer boy;
> Mother, press your lips to mine;
> O, they bring me peace and joy!
> 'Tis the last time on earth
> I shall ever see your face
> Mother take me to your heart,
> Let me die in your embrace . . .
>
> Farewell, mother, Death's cold hand
> Weighs upon my spirit now,
> And I feel his blighting breath
> Fan my pallid cheek and brow.
> Closer! closer! to your heart,
> Let me feel that you are by,
> While my sight is growing dim,
> For the dear old Flag I die.

In the Confederate States of America, the essential Southern anthem—"I Wish I Was in Dixie's Land"—was conceived, written, and first performed in New York, as part of a minstrel revue. And as so often happens with lasting pieces of music, it was composed hurriedly. In March 1859, Daniel Decatur Emmett, who was writing and performing for Bryant's Minstrels, was asked to produce a new number for a show. Emmett, a native of Ohio, complied, and "Dixie" was born. Verses and versions abound, but these words were, and are, fairly common to the song:

> I wish I was in the land of cotton,
> Old times there are not forgotten;
> Look away! Look away! Look away! Dixie Land.
> In Dixie's Land where I was born in,
> Early on one frosty mornin',
> Look away! Look away! Look away! Dixie Land.
>
> Then I wish I was in Dixie, Hooray! Hooray!
> In Dixie's Land I'll take my stand
> to live and die in Dixie.
> Away, away, away down south in Dixie.
> Away, away, away down south in Dixie.

That the song was written to be performed by blackface performers is a little-noted but vital fact. "Dixie" was composed by a white man and sung by whites who were pretending to be Blacks who were supposed to be pining nostalgically for the South. Context is all: minstrel singers on a New York stage suggesting that the "land of cotton" was preferable to the free North. The tune was popular in the North and in the South; Lincoln himself admired it.

The imperative to give the Confederacy a common sense of identity as it marched into war was evident even before Jefferson Davis's inauguration. In the Secession Winter, as Southern state after Southern state left the Union, Missis-

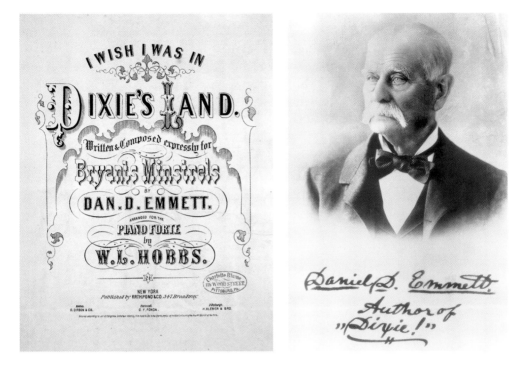

Written for the blackface minstrel stage in New York by Daniel Decatur Emmett (right), "I Wish I Was in Dixie's Land" became the anthem of the Confederate States of America.

sippi flew what became known as the "Bonnie Blue Flag," a blue banner with a single five-point star, as a replacement for the Stars and Stripes. Written by Harry Macarthy, a performer who was known as the "Arkansas Comedian," "The Bonnie Blue Flag" offered the Confederacy a kind of instant history. Macarthy also borrowed the Shakespearean image of a "band of brothers" from "Hail Columbia," writing:

I WISH I WAS IN DIXIE'S LAND

The history of "Dixie" is one of the reasons history is so important: I promise that there are precious few folks, North or South, who have much (or any) idea that the anthem of the Confederacy was written for blackface performers in New York City—or that Abraham Lincoln said it was one of his favorite tunes. In just those two details, you get a sense of the tangled complexity of America's story. For a lot of white Southerners, the song evokes warm memories of home; for a lot of African Americans, it's one more tragic reminder of the horrors of slavery and the all-too-persistent realities of racism.

And so I have to reconcile my memory of this song with its history and its purpose. I grew up in Northeast Louisiana, surrounded by cotton fields, on a street beside a cotton gin in the one-stoplight town of Start. My stepdad, Horace, was a truck driver who hauled cotton seed all over the Southeast, and I spent a lot of time as a kid riding along with him, listening to eight-track tapes of country-music icons Merle Haggard and George Jones. Those are some of my favorite childhood memories. Cotton and country music were how I grew up, so when I hear the refrain "I wish I was in the land of cotton . . . ," I sing along and think about my little postage stamp of earth, with a reflexive emotional longing to go back to the simplicity of being a kid in Louisiana.

Then, though, my brain kicks in, and I remember all that the song represents to so many others, and what history, not my heart, tells me it means. "Dixie" is an inescapable part of Southern and of American history, and I have no doubt that it portrays a proslavery point of view and relegates African Americans to the most un-American of places: a place where human beings are considered inferior because of the color of their skin and the circumstances of their birth. That may have been who we were, but it can't be who we are.

—T.M.

We are a band of brothers and native
 to the soil,
Fighting for the property we gained
 by honest toil;
And when our rights were
 threatened, the cry rose near and
 far,
Hurrah for the Bonnie Blue Flag
 that bears a single star!

Hurrah! Hurrah!
For Southern rights, hurrah!
Hurrah for the Bonnie Blue Flag
 that bears a single star.

As long as the Union was faithful to
 her trust,
Like friends and like brethren, kind
 were we, and just;

"The Bonnie Blue Flag," by the "Arkansas Comedian" Harry Macarthy, was an early attempt to find a unifying song for the states that were seceding from the Union.

But now, when Northern treachery attempts our rights to mar,
We hoist on high the Bonnie Blue Flag that bears a single star. . . .

Then here's to our Confederacy, strong we are and brave,
Like patriots of old we'll fight, our heritage to save;
And rather than submit to shame, to die we would prefer,
So cheer for the Bonnie Blue Flag that bears a single star.

"Like patriots of old": Such was a central claim of the Confederacy, that it, not the Union, represented the true principles of '76. As time went on, Macarthy

replaced the word "property" in the song's opening verse with "liberty" in order to minimize that the war was about slavery. By singing of "liberty," the rebels were better able to sustain the idea that they were at war to create a nation that was the real heir of the Founders—work that had fallen to men such as Thomas "Stonewall" Jackson, the Confederate hero, who was celebrated in "Stonewall Jackson's Way":

> He's in the saddle now! Fall in!
> Steady! The whole brigade!
> Hill's at the ford, cut off—we'll win
> His way out, ball and blade!
> What matter if our shoes are worn?
> What matter if our feet are torn?
> "Quick-step! We're with him before dawn!"
> That's "Stonewall Jackson's way." . . .
>
> Ah, maiden, wait, and watch, and yearn
> For news of Stonewall's band!
> Ah, widow, read, with eyes that burn,
> That ring upon thy hand!
> Ah, wife, sew on, pray on, hope on!
> Thy life shall not be all forlorn.
> The foe had better ne'er been born
> That gets in Stonewall's way.

On the other side of enemy lines, William Tecumseh Sherman's march through Georgia and the Carolinas inspired at least one enslaved community to sing a song that had been written as a Northern minstrel number by a white abolitionist, Henry Clay Work. Frightened by the coming of Union troops, a South

Carolina master fled. His enslaved population was more than a little amused. "My old master run off and stay in the woods a whole week when Sherman's men [came] through," Lorenza Ezell told a Works Progress Administration writer during the New Deal. He remembered their then singing a "funny song"—Henry Clay Work's:

> White folks, have you seen old master
> Up the road, with his
>   moustache on?
> He pick up his hat and he leave
>   real sudden
> And I believe he's up and gone.
>
> Old master run away
> And us darkies stay at home.
> It must be now that Kingdom's
>   comin'
> And the year of Jubilee.
>
> He look up the river and he
>   seen that smoke
> Where Lincoln's gunboats lay.
> He big enough and he old
>   enough and he ought to
>   know better,
> But he gone and run away.
>
> Now that overseer want to give
>   trouble
> And trot us 'round a spell,

After the Civil War, the cause of white supremacy replaced the defense of slavery as a consuming concern, and "Dixie" was seen in many quarters as a "patriotic song," despite its origins.

But we lock him up in the smokehouse cellar,
With the key done throwed in the well.

To Frederick Douglass, there had never been "a nobler and grander war than that which the loyal people of this country are now waging against the slave-holding rebels." In the end, the clash of arms and of ideas was the redemptive test of the American Revolution—the republic itself was on trial. At Gettysburg in 1863, President Lincoln spoke, as Douglass had, in the vernacular of the Declaration of Independence:

> Four score and seven years ago our fathers brought forth on this continent, a new nation, conceived in Liberty, and dedicated to the proposition that all men are created equal.
>
> Now we are engaged in a great civil war, testing whether that nation, or any nation so conceived and so dedicated, can long endure. We are met on a great battle-field of that war. We have come to dedicate a portion of that field, as a final resting place for those who here gave their lives that that nation might live. It is altogether fitting and proper that we should do this.
>
> But, in a larger sense, we cannot dedicate—we cannot consecrate—we cannot hallow—this ground. The brave men, living and dead, who struggled here, have consecrated it, far above our poor power to add or detract. The world will little note, nor long remember what we say here, but it can never forget what they did here.

A Union victory and the liberation of the enslaved would mean that America had, at least for a time, been delivered from evil in a day of "jubilee." The prospect of salvation—from sin in general and from slavery in particular—was the message of a favorite hymn of Frederick Douglass, "Blow Ye the Trumpet, Blow!":

> Blow ye the trumpet, blow,
> The gladly solemn sound,
> Let all the nations know
> To earth's remotest bound,
> The year of jubilee is come:
> Return, ye ransom'd sinners, home!
>
> Jesus, our great High-Priest,
> Hath full atonement made;
> Ye weary spirits rest,
> Ye mournful souls be glad,
> The year of jubilee is come:
> Return, ye ransom'd sinners, home! . . .
>
> Ye slaves of sin and hell,
> Your liberty receive,
> And safe in Jesus dwell,
> And bless'd in Jesus live:
> The year of jubilee is come:
> Return, ye ransom'd sinners, home!

With the Union's advantages and victories in the field, jubilee was at hand in the late winter and early spring of 1865. In his second inaugural, delivered on Saturday, March 4, 1865, however, Lincoln spoke more of tragedy than of triumph. He wanted victory—which would come thirty-six days later, with Lee's surrender to Grant at Appomattox—but he also longed for postbellum reunion and reconciliation. Speaking of both Northerners and Southerners, Lincoln mused: "Both read the same Bible and pray to the same God, and each invokes His aid against the other." Of slavery, the president noted: "It may seem strange that any men should dare to ask a just God's assistance in wringing their bread from the sweat of other men's faces, but let us judge not, that we be not judged." It was a conciliatory address, one that sought to acknowledge the ambiguity of history and the cosmic nature of the conflict.

In his "Song, On the Death of President Abraham Lincoln," published after Lincoln's assassination at Ford's Theatre, Silas S. Steele imagined an enduring role for Lincoln in the American story. Sung to the tune of "Annie Laurie," Steele's song said that Lincoln had been "Our Pilot and our Guide," and had "For Freedom lived and died." Going forward, Steele prayed:

> Let his Counsel still be nigh,
> And the Savior of our Union,
> Is with Washington on high.

Douglass deserves the last word on the war and on Lincoln, the man who often seems to loom largest over the history not only of the American presidency but of the nation. In 1876, Douglass said this as he dedicated a monument to the martyred president in Washington:

> It must be admitted, truth compels me to admit, even here in the presence of the monument we have erected to his memory, Abraham Lincoln was not, in the fullest sense of the word, either our man or our model. In his interests, in his associations, in his habits of thought and in his prejudices, he was a white man. . . .

> We are at best only his step-children; children by adoption, children by force of circumstances and necessity. . . . Our faith in him was often taxed and strained to the uttermost, but it never failed.

Douglass insisted that Lincoln must be considered wholly, not partially.

> Had he put the abolition of slavery before the salvation of the Union, he would have inevitably driven from him a powerful class of the American people and rendered resistance to rebellion impossible. Viewed from the genuine abolition ground, Mr. Lincoln seemed tardy, cold, dull, and indifferent; but measuring him by the sentiment of his country, a sentiment he was bound as a statesman to consult, he was swift, zealous, radical, and determined.

America would endure.

The country would march on, uncertainly and imperfectly and inconsistently. But at least it would march as one.

CHAPTER FOUR

MARCH, MARCH, MANY AS ONE

Daughters of freedom arise in your might!

—Suffrage Anthem, 1871

And we won't come back till it's over, over there.

—"Over There," by George M. Cohan, 1917

In the autumn of 1915, on a beautiful October day, more than twenty-five thousand marchers walked up Fifth Avenue in New York to the cheers, the *New York Times* reported, of a quarter of a million spectators. Thirty bands took part, playing different marching tunes, and there were fifteen thousand yellow banners on display. "The noise of traffic," the *Washington Post* wrote, gave "way to music mingled with the cheers of women." At dusk, fifteen bands joined together to play "The Star-Spangled Banner" at the Fifty-Ninth Street fountain at the entrance to Central Park. "As darkness fell," the *Post* reported, "the lights of shops still disclosed the seemingly endless lines of marchers, eight and sixteen abreast." The passage of the Nineteenth Amendment would finally come in time for the 1920 presidential election—a new day of jubilee.

The roots of the march could be said to stretch back to Abigail Adams and her admonition that the Founders "Remember the Ladies." As with the cause of

The suffrage leaders Susan B. Anthony and
Elizabeth Cady Stanton together in 1895.

independence in the Revolutionary War era and with abolition and secession in the years before and during the Civil War, songs offered a window on the feelings of the time. "Daughters of Freedom, the Ballot Be Yours" was published in 1871 and became a standard of the movement:

> Daughters of freedom arise in your might!
> March to the watchwords Justice and Right!
> Why will ye slumber? wake, O wake!
> Lo! on your legions light doth break!
> Sunder the fetters "custom" hath made!
> Come from the valley, hill and glade!
> Daughters of freedom, the truth marches on,
> Yield not the battle till ye have won!
> Heed not the "scorner," day by day
> Clouds of oppression roll away!

A watershed moment along the journey had come in the autumn of 1872, when the suffrage leader Susan B. Anthony opened her morning newspaper in Rochester, New York—and arose in her might.

The editorial, as she chose to read it, couldn't have been clearer. Perusing the Friday, November 1, 1872, edition of the *Rochester Democrat and Chronicle,* Susan B. Anthony took the words of the lead piece literally. "Now register!" the newspaper said. The presidential election was the next week, and the editors called on their readers to exercise the right to vote.

Anthony thought that a wonderful idea. The Eighth Ward's registry office doubled as a barbershop, and she gathered her three sisters and set out to follow the *Democrat and Chronicle*'s civic exhortation. "There was nothing," Anthony biographer Ida Husted Harper wrote, "to indicate that this appeal was made to

From Seneca Falls (the first women's rights convention held in the United States, in July 1848) to the Progressive era (a period of widespread social activism and political reform from the 1890s to the 1920s), the cause of women's suffrage was long, anguishing—but finally successful.

men only." Presenting herself to the ward's three registrars—two Republicans and one Democrat—Anthony saw their reluctance and then read them both the Fourteenth Amendment and the relevant article in the New York State Constitution—neither of which said anything about the franchise being limited to men only. Flummoxed, the officials "at length" accepted the Anthonys' registrations. (The Democrat dissented but was outvoted.)

The following Tuesday, Election Day, Anthony turned out early to cast her vote for Ulysses S. Grant in his contest against Horace Greeley. "Well I have been & gone & done it!!" she wrote to her friend and ally Elizabeth Cady Stanton.

"Positively voted the Republican ticket—straight—this AM at 7 o'clock and *swore my vote in at that.* . . . So we are in for a fine agitation in Rochester."

For daring to vote in Rochester in the 1872 election, Anthony was arrested, charged, and tried. When the marshal came to apprehend her, he was respectful, even bashful; with her sense of the dramatic, Anthony asked him to handcuff her. (He declined.) At her trial for illegally voting in a federal election, before Judge Ward Hunt in the United States Circuit Court for the Northern District of New York, Anthony was asked, after being convicted by an all-male jury, whether she had "anything to say." Anthony rose and addressed the court.

"Yes, your honor, I have many things to say; for in your ordered verdict of guilty, you have trampled under foot every vital principle of our government," Anthony said. "My natural rights, my civil rights, my political rights, my judicial rights, are all alike ignored. Robbed of the fundamental privilege of citizenship, I am degraded from the status of a citizen to that of a subject; and not only myself individually, but all of my sex, are, by your honor's verdict, doomed to political subjection under this, so-called, form of government."

Interrupting, the judge said: "The Court cannot listen to a rehearsal of arguments the prisoner's counsel has already consumed three hours in presenting."

Anthony pressed on until Judge Hunt cut her off. In the end, Anthony was fined one hundred dollars and court costs, but she refused to pay, and the government never collected.

Many of the women who'd fought for abolition—Harriet Tubman and Julia Ward Howe among them—now turned to suffrage.

That new movement had its own music. The suffragist Rebecca Naylor Hazard wrote the lyrics for "Give the Ballot to the Mothers," sung to the tune of "Marching Through Georgia." It echoed the Civil War's theme of deliverance in the language of "jubilee," with women's suffrage, not abolition, as the current goal:

Marchers heading up Fifth Avenue in New York City in a huge suffrage demonstration on Saturday, October 23, 1915.

Hurrah! hurrah! we bring the jubilee!
Hurrah! hurrah! the homes they shall be free!
So we'll sing the chorus from the mountains to the sea—
Giving the ballot to the mothers.

Bring the dear old banner, boys, and fling it to the wind;
Mother, wife and daughter, let it shelter and defend.
"Equal Rights" our motto is, we're loyal to the end—
Giving the ballot to the mothers.

It was a big, bold, contradictory time. As the twentieth century dawned, the nation had been growing both in scale and in ambition. In addition to suffrage, the

Progressive movements addressed the excesses of the Gilded Age, and by 1917, the nation would be at war in Europe in a convulsive struggle, with far-ranging implications at home and abroad. The America that had gone to war was undergoing seismic changes as the country became more urban, more diverse, and more engaged in the broader world. And there was, inevitably, fierce reaction to rising immigration, a foreign war, agitation for women's suffrage, and persistent pleas for an end to Jim Crow. The century's first decades gave us the NAACP and the American Civil Liberties Union—and, not coincidentally, a revived Ku Klux Klan, which began a reign of terror at its refounding at Stone Mountain, Georgia, in the autumn of 1915.

The Klan was the most dramatic manifestation of white anxiety about the shifting nature of the nation. While women marched, African Americans fought, too, for a rightful portion of the American promise. "The principle of racial and class equality is at the basis of American political life," said Jane Addams, a leader in the history of social work and women's suffrage in the United States. "And to wantonly destroy it is one of the gravest outrages against the Republic."

And yet here was a great truth: Appomattox had been a beginning, not an ending, as white Southerners, often abetted, explicitly and implicitly, by whites in the North, secured legalized segregation after the Union victory. In the wake of the war, the Virginia Confederate and journalist Edward Alfred Pollard argued for the defense of the "Lost Cause" of white supremacy. The issue was no longer slavery but white dominance, which Pollard described as the "true cause of the war" and the "true hope of the South." The focus: the reassertion of states' rights and the rejection of federal rule.

Many white Americans had feared a postslavery society in which emancipation might lead to equality, and they ensured that no such thing should come to

"The battle we wage," W. E. B. Du Bois said of civil rights, "is not for ourselves alone but for all true Americans."

pass, North or South. Against terrible odds and through gloomy years, reformers continued to wage their long war to overcome racial injustice as the twentieth century began. In 1905, a group led by Du Bois met at Niagara, New York, to issue a declaration of principles. "We will not be satisfied to take one jot or tittle less than our full manhood rights," Du Bois said at the movement's second annual meeting at Harpers Ferry the next year. "The battle we wage is not for ourselves alone but for all true Americans. It is a fight for ideals, lest this, our common fatherland, false to its founding, become in truth the land of the thief and the home of the Slave—a byword and a hissing among the nations for its sounding pretensions and pitiful accomplishment."

Note the allusion to the language of Francis Scott Key: "land of the thief" (not "the free") and the "home of the Slave" (not "the brave"). "The Star-Spangled Banner," like the Declaration of Independence, was seen as a promissory American text, and, like the women suffragists, the Niagara Movement, as the effort

Founded in 1905, the Niagara Movement for racial equality helped lead to the creation of the NAACP.

became known, was calling on the nation to live up to its sacred founding document. "The morning breaks over blood-stained hills," Du Bois said at Harpers Ferry. "We must not falter, we may not shrink. Above are the everlasting stars."

Poetic words, but more-lasting poetry, written by James Weldon Johnson, was in circulation in African American circles. Johnson was the author of the lyrics to "Lift Every Voice and Sing"; his brother, J. Rosamond Johnson, composed the music. The Johnsons had produced the piece for a Lincoln's Birthday celebration in Jacksonville, Florida, in 1900, where five hundred schoolchildren sang the song. "Shortly afterwards my brother and I moved away from Jacksonville

The composers Bob Cole, James Weldon Johnson, and J. Rosamond Johnson; the Johnsons created "Lift Every Voice and Sing," which became known as the "Negro National Hymn."

to New York, and the song passed out of our minds," James Weldon Johnson recalled. "But the school children of Jacksonville kept singing it; they went off to other schools and sang it; they became teachers and taught it to other children. Within twenty years it was being sung over the South and in some other parts of the country. Today the song, popularly known as the Negro National Hymn, is quite generally used":

> Lift every voice and sing
> Till earth and heaven ring,
> Ring with the harmonies of Liberty;
> Let our rejoicing rise
> High as the listening skies,
> Let it resound loud as the rolling sea.
> Sing a song full of the faith that the dark past has taught us,
> Sing a song full of the hope that the present has brought us.
> Facing the rising sun of our new day begun,
> Let us march on till victory is won.

An image from the twentieth annual meeting of the NAACP, held in 1929; W. E. B. Du Bois and James Weldon Johnson are pictured on the bottom row, fifth and sixth from the left.

Stony the road we trod,

Bitter the chastening rod,

Felt in the days when hope unborn had died;

Yet with a steady beat,

Have not our weary feet

Come to the place for which our fathers sighed?

We have come over a way that with tears has been watered,

We have come, treading our path through the blood of the slaughtered,

Out from the gloomy past,

Till now we stand at last

Where the white gleam of our bright star is cast.

God of our weary years,

God of our silent tears,

Thou who hast brought us thus far on the way;

Thou who hast by Thy might

Led us into the light,

Keep us forever in the path, we pray.

Lest our feet stray from the places, our God, where we met Thee,

Lest our hearts drunk with the wine of the world, we forget Thee;

Shadowed beneath Thy hand,

May we forever stand.

True to our God,

True to our native land.

The song's success was organic. "I have commonly found printed or typewritten copies of the words pasted in the back of hymnals and the song books used in Sunday schools, Y.M.C.A.s and similar institutions and I think that is the manner by which it gets its widest circulation," Johnson recalled. "Nothing I have done has paid me back so fully as being part creator of this song." Du Bois, who had helped found the NAACP in 1909, met Johnson in 1916, and by 1919 the organization had made Johnson's song its official hymn.

★★★★★★★★★★★★★★★★★★★★★★★★★★★★★★★

LIFT EVERY VOICE AND SING

This song's been cherished by the civil rights movement in its several incarnations. Written early in the twentieth century to commemorate Abraham Lincoln's birthday, it became known as the "Negro National Hymn." Sixty years after its composition, it was still cherished and sung in the movement of the 1950s and 1960s. After so much misrepresentation and exploitation of Black people with minstrelsy and the pain of so many spirituals and hymns, I can see how this song finally felt like a proud representation of African American art, culture, and history.

Music makes us feel *seen,* and this song allowed a new image of African Americans to be seen within and without Black culture. The lyrics acknowledge the past but sketch a hopeful picture of the future. Modern performers— from Beyoncé at the Coachella festival (where she was the first Black woman to headline the event) to Aloe Blacc at Super Bowl LIII—continue to keep the song and its message alive. —T.M.

It is a song of tempered hope. It assumes that the present is better than the past and prays that the future may be better yet. Johnson's verses express, too, a faith in America itself—a "native land" to which we owe allegiance.

At the March on Washington in August 1963, Benjamin Mays, the president of Morehouse College, quoted "Lift Every Voice" in his benediction. And a century after the founding of the NAACP, the Reverend Joseph Lowery recited the final verse of Johnson's song while offering the closing prayer at the 2009 inauguration of Barack Obama.

It was a busy day. On Wednesday, May 1, 1940, President Franklin D. Roosevelt drafted a letter to King George VI, stopped off for a visit with the White House doctor, and looked forward to lunch with Sumner Welles, the under secretary of state. There was much to think about, and to discuss. Adolf Hitler's Wehrmacht had struck Norway and was on the verge of its blitzkrieg through Western Europe. The invasion of France and of the Low Countries had been secretly scheduled for the next week. London was in chaos. "These have indeed been most crowded days & I have had to do my utmost to keep pace with the ceaseless flow of telegrams," Winston Churchill, then Great Britain's First Lord of the Admiralty, wrote during the assault on Norway. Churchill had held the same office during World War I, the "Great War," two decades before, in the same years in

"Over There": American soldiers along the Western Front, the scene of terrible trench warfare in World War I.

which the young Roosevelt had served as assistant secretary of the Navy. The two were both transported back to the old cataclysm in the midst of the new.

The Great War was very much on the president's mind on this springtime Wednesday in Washington. At 11:30 A.M., FDR presented the Congressional Gold Medal to George M. Cohan, the vaudevillian, performer, composer, and author of several songs that had played a role in the war effort in World War I under Roosevelt's old chief, Woodrow Wilson. Cohan had starred as Roosevelt on Broadway in a production called *I'd Rather Be Right,* and the cheerful president called out, "Well, how's my double?" as Cohan came into the Oval Office.

The medal had been authorized, as the *New York Times* headline put it, in recognition of Cohan's "old war songs"—songs that had brought the always-fractious country together in 1917-18 and that were resonant again in 1940. Cohan's "I'm a Yankee Doodle Boy," for instance, had been popular during the Great War.

> I'm a Yankee Doodle Dandy,
> A Yankee Doodle, do or die;
> A real live nephew of my Uncle Sam's,
> Born on the Fourth of July.

Like Francis Scott Key a century or so before, Cohan had also drawn inspiration from the Stars and Stripes in "You're a Grand Old Flag":

> You're a grand old flag
> You're a high-flying flag
> And forever in peace may you wave
>
> You're the emblem of the land I love
> The home of the free and the brave

Every heart beats true under Red, White,
  and Blue
Where there's never a boast or brag
"But should old acquaintance be forgot"
Keep your eye on the grand old flag.

In awarding the gold medal, Congress singled out Cohan's "Over There," an anthem that played on the existing language of patriotism. It evoked the American Revolution's "Yankee Doodle," employed the Revolutionary phrase "Son of Liberty," and added the imagery of global mission for a country long defined by its distance from the Old World:

Johnny, get your gun, get your gun, get
  your gun.
Take it on the run, on the run, on the run.
Hear them calling you and me,
Every son of liberty.
Hurry right away, no delay, go today.
Make your daddy glad to have had such a
  lad.
Tell your sweetheart not to pine
To be proud her boy's in line.

Johnny, get your gun, get your gun, get
  your gun.

George M. Cohan's songs became immensely popular in wartime.

Johnny, show the "Hun" you're a son-of-a-gun.
Hoist the flag and let her fly
Yankee Doodle do or die.
Pack your little kit, show your grit, do your bit.
Yankee to the ranks from the towns and the tanks.
Make your mother proud of you
And the old red-white-and-blue

Over there, over there,
Send the word, send the word over there
That the Yanks are coming, the Yanks are coming
The drums rum-tumming everywhere
So prepare, say a prayer,
Send the word, send the word to beware—
We'll be over, we're coming over,
And we won't come back till it's over, over there.

Cohan had written most of it in a burst in New York City and at his house in Great Neck, Long Island, after reading the headlines about Woodrow Wilson's declaration of war. Calling his family together, Cohan announced that he had a new song. "So we all sat down and waited expectantly because we always loved to hear him sing," Cohan's daughter, Mary, recalled. "He put a big tin pan from the kitchen on his head, used a broom for a gun on his shoulder, and he started to mark time like a soldier," as he broke into the words of "Over There."

Musing about his audience with FDR years later, Cohan recalled, "Funny about them giving me a medal. All I wrote was a bugle call. I read those war headlines and I got to thinking and to humming to myself. . . ." But, of course, "Over There" was more than a bugle call. It was an inspired, and inspiring, song of resolve and of duty—"show your grit, do your bit"; "Make your mother proud of you."

The lyrics spoke, too, to an American sense of identity—a vision of the nation's role as a universal force for good.

The Great War itself gave rise to protest, a strain of sentiment embodied in 1915's "I Didn't Raise My Boy to Be a Soldier," a song written by Alfred Bryan and marketed, in sheet music, as "A Mother's Plea for Peace":

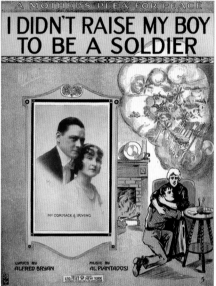

Subtitled "A Mother's Plea for Peace," "I Didn't Raise My Boy to Be a Soldier" was an early piece of protest music.

> I didn't raise my boy to be a soldier,
> I brought him up to be my pride and joy,
> Who dares to place a musket on his
>   shoulder,
> To shoot some other mother's darling
>   boy?
> Let nations arbitrate their future
>   troubles,
> It's time to lay the sword and gun away,
> There'd be no war today,
> If mothers all would say,
> "I didn't raise my boy to be a soldier."

OVER THERE and I DIDN'T RAISE MY BOY
TO BE A SOLDIER

"Over There" is a classic patriotic song from the great world wars. Listening to the original version by Billy Murray, I found it to be incredibly positive and uplifting—which, of course, was George M. Cohan's goal. War, as General Sherman said, is hell, and music is often one of the few tools that commanders and soldiers can deploy to remind them of why they're out there—or "over there"—risking everything.

Speaking of which: I simply can't imagine the pain a mother must feel at losing a son (or daughter) in war. "I Didn't Raise My Boy to Be a Soldier" is a forerunner to all the iconic antiwar music of the 1960s. This song brings home the real impact of the decision to go to war. It's not all about parades and glory; at heart, combat is brutal, and every soldier who falls lives on in the hearts of those who loved him (or, in the twenty-first century, her). Musically, it's intriguing that the song has the feel of a march juxtaposed against the message of peace in the lyrics. While melodically I'm called to battle, lyrically I'm called to contemplate the price that's to be paid for waging war.

—T.M.

For all the difficulties of the age, there was always hope. After World War I, the poet Katharine Lee Bates, the author of "America the Beautiful," was told that American soldiers at Verdun, the scene of unspeakably bloody trench warfare, had marked the Armistice by singing her verses. The news brought tears to her eyes.

Katharine Lee Bates believed her poem "America the Beautiful," set to "Materna" by Samuel A. Ward, endured because "Americans are at heart idealists."

★★★★★★★★★★★★★★★★★★★★★★★★★★★★★★★★

AMERICA THE BEAUTIFUL

The poetry of the lyrics is so visual: amber, purple, alabaster. This is one of those songs that can take you from the dark to the light in an instant, not least because of the colors Katharine Lee Bates evokes in her writing. Multiple melodies have been placed over the words through time, and it lends itself to so many interpretations on a musical level.

Bates's aesthetic sensibility clearly informed her verses. And she was a tough woman. In a tiny red notebook she kept as a girl, she wrote, "Girls are a very necessary portion of creation. They are full as necessary as boys. . . . Boys don't do much but outdore work. Girls work is all in doors. It isn't fair."

It wasn't, and it began to change because of the suffrage movement led by women like Elizabeth Cady Stanton and Susan B. Anthony, among so many others. It's a movement that's still going, part of the unfinished work of the country.

—T.M.

Composed after an excursion to Pikes Peak outside Colorado Springs in the Rocky Mountains in 1895, "America the Beautiful" had been set to the music of "Materna," by Samuel A. Ward.

O beautiful for spacious skies,
For amber waves of grain,
For purple mountain majesties,
Above the fruited plain!
America! America!
God shed His grace on thee
And crown thy good with brotherhood
From sea to shining sea!

O beautiful for pilgrim feet,
Whose stern, impassioned stress
A thoroughfare for freedom beat
Across the wilderness!
America! America!
God mend thine every flaw,
Confirm thy soul in self-control,
Thy liberty in law!

O beautiful for heroes proved
In liberating strife,
Who more than self their country loved,
And mercy more than life!
America! America!
May God thy gold refine

Till all success be nobleness,
And every gain divine!

O beautiful for patriot dream
That sees beyond the years
Thine alabaster cities gleam
Undimmed by human tears!
America! America!
God shed His grace on thee
And crown thy good with brotherhood
From sea to shining sea!

In 2016, Barack Obama would tell the *New Yorker*'s David Remnick that Ray Charles's version of "America the Beautiful" would, for him, "always be . . . the most patriotic piece of music ever performed—because it captures the fullness of the American experience, the view from the bottom as well as the top, the good and the bad, and the possibility of synthesis, reconciliation, transcendence."

Charles himself had a similarly complex understanding of the piece. "Remember, I got to first feel the music, do somethin' with the song," Charles told *Rolling Stone* in an interview published in 1973. "And that's why in that album you have a song like 'America.' . . . I love this country, man. And I wouldn't live in no place else. You understand. My family was born here. My great-grandparents were born here. I think I got as much roots in this country as anybody else. So I think when somethin's wrong, it's up to me to try to change it. I was sayin' that America is a beautiful country. It's just some of our policies that people don't dig."

Bates would have likely agreed. "That the hymn has gained . . . such a hold as it has upon our people," she remarked, "is clearly due to the fact that Americans are at heart idealists, with a fundamental faith in human brotherhood." That idealism was under constant challenge, but Bates was onto something: Only by staying on freedom's thoroughfare can our patriot dreams ever move from the ideal to the real.

Marian Anderson sings from the steps of the Lincoln Memorial on Easter Sunday 1939; seventy-five thousand people flocked to the National Mall to hear her.

CHAPTER FIVE

AS THE STORM CLOUDS GATHER

I've seen the dust so black I couldn't see a thing.
—WOODY GUTHRIE, on the Dust Bowl and the Great Depression in the song
"Dust Bowl Blues"

Songs make history and history makes songs.
—IRVING BERLIN, on the coming of World War II

A voice one hears once in a hundred years.
—ARTURO TOSCANINI, on Marian Anderson

The city was thronged. On Thursday, September 3, 1936, tens of thousands of people lined the streets of Des Moines, Iowa, to catch a glimpse of President Franklin D. Roosevelt, who arrived by train at the Rock Island station at noon. Troops from the Fourteenth Cavalry stood at attention as uniformed buglers greeted the commander in chief, who emerged from *Pioneer,* his private carriage, balanced on the arm of his youngest son, John Roosevelt. Smiling broadly and waving to a cheering crowd, Roosevelt was transferred to an open car, where he sat next to the governor of Iowa and the mayor of Des Moines. Their destination: a meeting of Midwestern and Plains governors at the state capitol to discuss drought relief—a summit that included Roosevelt's opponent

The author of "God Bless America," Irving Berlin, seen here playing for American soldiers, was a vital composer in both world wars.

in the coming presidential election, Alf M. Landon of Kansas. The presence of the two major-party candidates in Des Moines, which was already unusually full because of the late-summer Iowa State Fair, created an electric atmosphere. 100,000 JAM CITY TO CHEER NOMINEES, the *Washington Post* reported. Police sirens blared as the president's motorcade inched its way through the city's business district. As the president rode along, he waved his Panama hat to acknowledge the spectators, some of whom, the *New York Times* wrote, were standing six deep. Ticker tape came down in bursts, and the crowds were in what the *Times* called a "holiday spirit."

Such was Roosevelt's magnetism and power—a magnetism and a power on vivid display on that September Thursday in Des Moines, roughly seven years into the Great Depression.

Nearly half a century later, at least one admirer could recall FDR's parade from the train station to the capitol in great detail. A young sportscaster at Des Moines's WHO radio station had been visibly thrilled as he hurried to the window of his offices on Walnut Street to take in the motorcade. "Franklin Roosevelt was the first president I ever saw," Ronald Reagan told a gathering of Roosevelt family and New Dealers at a 1982 centennial celebration of the thirty-second president's birth. "What a wave of affection and pride swept through that crowd as he passed by in an open car . . . a familiar smile on his lips, jaunty and confident, drawing from us reservoirs of confidence and enthusiasm some of us had forgotten we had during those hard years. Maybe that was FDR's greatest gift to us. He really did convince us that the only thing we had to fear was fear itself."

Speaking in the East Room, Reagan, now the fortieth president, paid tribute to the Democrat for whom he had voted four times—in 1932, 1936, 1940, and 1944. "FDR was denounced by some as a traitor to his class," Reagan said. "But people who said that missed the whole point of what he believed in and what this country's all about. There's only one class and that's 'We, the People.'" The sight of Roosevelt in Des Moines, Reagan recalled, was when he had "first felt the awe and majesty of this office."

Reagan had grown more conservative in the 1950s and early '60s and had changed parties. At his inauguration in January 1981, amid high inflation and interest rates, Reagan had denounced the growth of the federal establishment—growth that had begun under FDR—and said: "In this present crisis, government is not the solution to our problem; government is the problem."

Yet there was no such talk in the East Room as Reagan warmly remembered FDR. "This great nation of ours is a caring, loving land," Reagan said. "Its people have a zest for life and laughter, and Franklin Roosevelt shared those qualities. But we're also a practical people with an inborn sense of proportion. We sense when things have gone too far, when the time has come to make fundamental

Affirming his faith in the future, FDR addressed the Democratic National Convention in Chicago in 1932—the gathering that gave the party its theme song "Happy Days Are Here Again."

changes. Franklin Roosevelt was that kind of a person, too." FDR, in other words, belonged not to the past but to the present and to the future. The president then offered a toast: to "Happy days—now, again, and always."

The reference was unmistakable, for Franklin Roosevelt and the song "Happy Days Are Here Again" were inseparable in the political imaginations of Americans conversant with the years of what the historian Arthur M. Schlesinger, Jr., called "The Age of Roosevelt." Written by Jack Yellin, with music by Milton Ager, the song had been created before the October 1929 stock market crash, for an MGM movie called *Chasing Rainbows,* which was released in early 1930.

The public heard it in the context of hard economic times, and, as historians have noted, the song's "seemingly upbeat lyrics laughed off the Depression; better days had to be coming."

The song entered the nation's political consciousness at the Democratic National Convention at the Chicago Stadium in 1932, which had also been the site of the Republican convention. The venue's organist, Al Melgard, had prepared and played "Happy Days Are Here Again" for both conventions, but, as Donald A. Ritchie pointed out in an account of the 1932 campaign, "The song's bouncy rhythm seemed out of sync with the somber Republican proceedings and went unnoticed." Roosevelt, who was seeking the presidential nomination, had planned to have "Anchors Aweigh" as his theme song, reminding delegates and listeners on the radio of his tenure as assistant secretary of the Navy during the Great War. From his command post at the Congress Hotel, Roosevelt adviser Louis Howe listened to his secretary, a fan of "Happy Days Are Here Again," sing it out for him. Impressed, the wizened politico sent word to the hall to change course: "Happy Days Are Here Again" was now the FDR standard.

A fitting choice, for insistent optimism was one of Roosevelt's great gifts to the country. By 1932, the Great Depression had consumed the United States, and in accepting the presidential nomination at the Democratic National Convention in Chicago that July, FDR addressed himself to the future. "The greatest tribute that I can pay to my countrymen is that in these days of crushing want there persists an orderly and hopeful spirit on the part of the millions of our people who have suffered so much," Roosevelt said. "I pledge you, I pledge myself, to a New Deal for the American people."

Roosevelt refused to concede that America's day was past. "This great Nation will endure as it has endured, will revive and will prosper," he told the country after taking the oath of office on Saturday, March 4, 1933. "So, first of all, let me assert my firm belief that the only thing we have to fear is fear itself—nameless, unreasoning, unjustified terror which paralyzes needed efforts to convert retreat into advance."

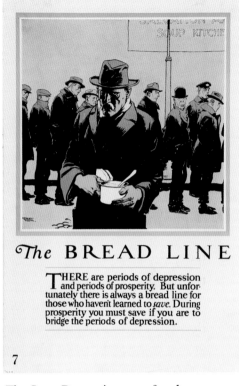

ᐒhe BREAD LINE

THERE are periods of depression and periods of prosperity. But unfortunately there is always a bread line for those who haven't learned to *save*. During prosperity you must save if you are to bridge the periods of depression.

The Great Depression was of such scope that "Brother, Can You Spare a Dime?" had a tragically wide resonance.

Roosevelt's show of confidence required immense effort, for no one—including the president himself—truly knew if the skies above would be blue again. In the popular "Brother, Can You Spare a Dime?" (Bing Crosby sang a successful version, released in 1932; the music was by Jay Gorney with lyrics by E. Y. "Yip" Harburg), the narrator is an unemployed veteran of the Great War—a man who has done his bit, played by the rules, kept his end of the bargain, and yet is now in a bread line, begging for the money he used to earn but, through no fault of his own, now can't. Plaintive and sad, the song was grimly applicable to innumerable shattered lives. The task that fell to Roosevelt: to rescue a nation torn between the hope of "Happy Days Are Here Again" and the soul-crushing reality of "Brother, Can You Spare a Dime?"

★★★★★★★★★★★★★★★★★★★★★★★★★★★★★★

BROTHER, CAN YOU SPARE A DIME?

So melancholy—this one always hits me hard, especially the Bing Crosby version. It's about powerlessness and broken promises, which is what so many enduring songs are about. The narrator did everything he was supposed to do but the world failed him anyway, and that's where politics so often comes in, because if We the People can't help out individual people in trouble, then the fabric of the country frays.

I never considered myself poor growing up, but we definitely had to stretch to make ends meet. This song makes me think of all the times my mother fought to keep food on the table and how difficult it must have been to keep her spirits up. The thought of anyone who wants to work and provide for their family but can't absolutely tears me up. And it should tear all of us up.   —T.M.

Woody Guthrie spoke to that "Can You Spare a Dime?" sphere of discontent in America. Born in Oklahoma in 1912, Guthrie was a wanderer, a folk philosopher, and one of the great American songwriter-musicians. "A song," he once said, "ain't nothing but a conversation fixed up to where you can talk it over and over without getting tired of it." He sang of the Dust Bowl and of broken lives, of fear and of endurance, depicting the Depression as an event on a scale with Armageddon. "I've seen the dust so black," Guthrie sang in "Dust Bowl Blues," "that I couldn't see a thing."

In 1938, the drift toward chaos and bloodshed in Europe prompted the composer Irving Berlin to excavate a song he'd written in 1918, "God Bless Amer-

During the Great Depression, the Dust Bowl devastated many lives amid drought, economic hardship, and lost hope.

ica." He arranged for the singer Kate Smith to perform it on her CBS radio show on Armistice Day 1938, and Smith would record the number in early 1939. (In 2019, news of her having sung "That's Why Darkies Were Born" and "Pickaninny Heaven" led the New York Yankees and the Philadelphia Flyers to ban her rendition of "God Bless America.") In the late 1930s, fearing Hitler, listeners did not have to think hard about what she meant when she spoke of "the storm clouds" gathering "far across the sea" or "the night" that required "a light from above."

Guthrie, though, heard something else in Berlin's verses: a triumphalism that portrayed America simplistically and sentimentally. And so Guthrie wrote a reply. Initially entitled "God Blessed America," it became "This Land Is Your Land," a song that grew in popularity during and after World War II. The language of the song was fluid, but one verse said:

Woody Guthrie's "This Land Is Your Land" was written in response to "God Bless America"—an example of the perennial American debate about the country's promise and reality.

In the shadow of the steeple I saw my people,
By the relief office I seen my people;
As they stood there hungry, I stood there asking
Is this land made for you and me?

It was a query that subsequent generations would repeatedly pose. The verse, however, has often been omitted from widely published and frequently sung versions of the song. Another pointed lyric about a "big high wall" with a "Private Property" sign—an image of capitalistic coldness—also slipped into the mists. Why is a bit of a mystery, but the lyrics were perhaps thought too provocative for the broad public. Pete Seeger, an artistic heir to the Guthrie tradition, was praised for singing what are sometimes called the "forbidden verses" during a concert celebrating Barack Obama's inauguration in 2009.

*   *   *

The war to bring the country closer to fulfilling the promise of the declaration was a longtime concern of Eleanor Roosevelt. The niece of one president and the wife of another, Mrs. Roosevelt was a tireless reformer, often pressing her husband to go further, faster, on issues of social justice, including civil rights.

THIS LAND IS YOUR LAND

Woody Guthrie was to rock and roll what Hank Williams, Sr., was to country music. He was a singer-songwriter in the way we think of it today, especially in country music, with a guitar in hand, scribbling lyrics on a notepad. It sounds simple, but lyrically he's singing with a cause and a message— a rebellion that would fuel those who came after, like Bob Dylan and Bruce Springsteen.

Guthrie was born in Oklahoma, and he was part of the great Dust Bowl Migration west, locating in California. He would ultimately move east to New York and begin to build his legacy as one of the greatest folk artists and writers. During World War II, he supported the cause by performing his songs, often on an acoustic guitar with a sticker that said THIS MACHINE KILLS FASCISTS.

The Dust Bowl Migration greatly influenced Guthrie's outlook on the world and his songwriting. In "This Land Is Your Land," he's survived that mighty struggle, and he's come to realize its vast beauty and bounty.

But he knows, too, that all is not perfect and may never be. His music is testament to the work that we all have to do, whether it's with a guitar or with the ballot.   —T.M.

One of her causes was anti-lynching legislation to address the brutality of extralegal white murders of African Americans. Despite her pressure, Congress, dominated by white Southern Democrats, never enacted measures to curb the mob violence that killed an estimated 3,500 African Americans between 1882 and 1968. Moved by reports of these murders, a New York City schoolteacher, Abel Meeropol, crafted a poem, "Strange Fruit," which Billie Holiday recorded in 1939. "I wrote 'Strange Fruit,'" Meeropol recalled, "because I hate lynching and I hate injustice and I hate the people who perpetuate it." It was an explicit, moving depiction of the horrors of lynching in the South.

Around the time Holiday was first singing "Strange Fruit" in the Café Society nightclub in Greenwich Village, the Daughters of the American Revolution refused to allow the singer Marian Anderson to perform at the organization's Constitution Hall, not far from the White House. The DAR's venue, the group said, was for "white artists" only. Mrs. Roosevelt, a member of the organization,

Eleanor Roosevelt resigned from the Daughters of the American Revolution after the organization refused to allow Marian Anderson (right) to perform at Washington's Constitution Hall.

resigned from the DAR in protest, writing in her My Day newspaper column: "To remain as a member implies approval of that action, therefore I am resigning." When Anderson was told of the First Lady's resignation, the singer said, "I am not surprised at Mrs. Roosevelt's action, because she seems to me to be one who really comprehends the true meaning of democracy."

An alternative plan took shape: The Interior Department, under Secretary Harold Ickes, would invite Anderson to sing at the Lincoln Memorial. "I don't care if she sings from the top of the Washington Monument," FDR said, "as long as she sings."

An African American who had won global acclaim, Anderson had "a voice one hears once in a hundred years," remarked the great conductor Arturo Toscanini. Born in Philadelphia in 1897, Anderson was dignity itself. Asked in later years about the controversy, she declined to attack the DAR for its discriminatory decision. "Music to me means so much, such beautiful things," she said, "and it seemed impossible that you could find people who would curb you, stop you, from doing a thing which is beautiful."

The concert was planned for 5:00 P.M. on Easter Sunday, April 9, 1939. Anderson's management and civil rights advocates joined forces, and much of official Washington lent its support to the effort. "In this great auditorium under the sky, all of us are free," Harold Ickes said in introducing Anderson to a national radio audience. "When God gave us this wonderful outdoors and the sun, the moon and the stars, He made no distinction of race, or creed, or color."

The sun broke through the clouds as Anderson sang. In a remarkable tableau, seventy-five thousand people had come to hear the concert, and the image of an African American standing in the same frame with Lincoln to sing of the "sweet land of liberty" was historic, stirring, *hopeful.*

MY SOUL'S BEEN ANCHORED IN THE LORD and HE'S GOT THE WHOLE WORLD IN HIS HANDS

Marian Anderson was one of the finest singers—male or female—in American history. She was a thread between her Easter Sunday 1939 concert and the 1963 March on Washington; she sang "My Soul's Been Anchored in the Lord" at the first and "He's Got the Whole World in His Hands" at the second. I connect with the anchor theme in "My Soul's Been Anchored in the Lord." Here African American music has gone from the spiritual, which was more about getting through, to the political, with music as an instrument of social change. Their struggle may be mighty, but so is their anchor: "Until I reach the mountaintop . . . my soul is anchored." Anchored in the mountaintop. Glorious.

I imagine a lot of folks' first encounter with these songs was in the church. Both African American spirituals, they moved from the pews and the choirs to the people and the capital. And as a parent, the thing that really stands out for me with "He's Got the Whole World in His Hands" is how this song has become a song for our children. Its sing-along verses with a single hook line repeated over and over make it easy for everyone to join together, lifting voices in praise.

—T.M.

"It was a tour de force that stirred and sensitized the national psyche to the reality of racial discrimination, even as it symbolized bedrock American values," the *Washington Post*'s Bart Barnes wrote in a 1993 obituary of Anderson. And the afternoon came to loom large in the history of the fight for racial equality.

* * *

By the last day of January 1939, just over two months before the Anderson concert, FDR had become convinced that, as he put it, there was "a policy of world domination between Germany, Italy, and Japan." That August, Hitler and Joseph Stalin concluded a mutual nonaggression pact, thus freeing Hitler to strike Poland and westward, which he did beginning on the first day of September 1939.

May 1940 was a critical month. On Friday, May 10, Winston Churchill became Great Britain's prime minister at the grimmest of moments. "I felt as if I were walking with Destiny," Churchill recalled of his arrival at the pinnacle, "and that all my past life had been but a preparation for this hour and for this trial." In Washington, Roosevelt was less certain. Churchill was seen as a drinker, as an adventurer, as a sentimentalist. Harold Ickes recalled that in a cabinet meeting that momentous Friday, the president said that he "supposed Churchill was the best man that England had, even if he was drunk half of his time."

On Thursday, May 23, 1940, Arthur Schlesinger, Jr., wrote in his journal, "Hitler is not a mere imperialist conqueror, but moved essentially by economic needs and governed by considerations of expediency. His war is not a war for markets and colonies. It is a revolution and a crusade. . . . [Hitler] is the prophet of a new religion, and like all prophets is out to convert or destroy. It is democracy or Nazism."

Roosevelt, however, did not believe America was ready to do much of anything for Britain. A poll in this period, William L. Langer and S. Everett Gleason wrote in their 1952 study, *The Challenge to Isolation,* "indicated that only 7.7 percent of the population was in favor of entering the war at once and only 19 percent believed that the country should intervene if the defeat of the Allies appeared certain, as against 40 percent that *opposed American participation under any circumstances*" [emphasis added]. These were thought to be the quarrels of other people, far away.

*　*　*

While Roosevelt was constrained by the times, Churchill faced the exigencies of circumstance in a much more immediate way. Confronted with the collapse of France and the prospect of an invasion of England itself, the prime minister rallied the nation on Tuesday, June 4, 1940:

> Even though large tracts of Europe and many old and famous States have fallen or may fall into the grip of the Gestapo and all the odious apparatus of Nazi rule, we shall not flag or fail. We shall go on to the end.

After the Battle of Britain, the American Walter Kent composed a song, with lyrics by Nat Burton, to commemorate the defense of liberty in the skies over the English Channel. "(There'll Be Bluebirds Over) The White Cliffs of Dover" spoke of combat and captured the human longing for freedom and for peace.

The Battle of Britain in 1940 was, in Churchill's phrase, his nation's "finest hour."

*　*　*

Sacred music brought Churchill and Roosevelt together. In August 1941, at Placentia Bay off Newfoundland, Roosevelt and Churchill rendezvoused in secret to talk over the war—a war that the United States had not yet entered. At a Sunday morning service aboard the HMS *Prince of Wales,* the British prime minister did all he could to create a shared sense of mission with the president by drawing on their common Anglican vernacular. "I have," Churchill remarked beforehand, "chosen some grand hymns." Together with the assembled sailors, the president and the prime minister sat in the sea air and sang:

> O God, our help in ages past,
> Our hope for years to come,
> Our shelter from the stormy blast,
> And our eternal home . . .

There was the General Confession, the Lord's Prayer, and then the second hymn:

> Onward, Christian soldiers,
> Marching as to war,
> With the cross of Jesus
> Going on before!
> Christ, the Royal Master,
> Leads against the foe;
> Forward into battle,
> See, his banners go . . .

There was a reading from the Book of Joshua: "Be not afraid: for the Lord thy God is with thee whithersoever thou goest." More prayers followed, then a final hymn:

Eternal Father, strong to save,

Whose arm hath bound the restless wave,

Who bidd'st the mighty ocean deep

Its own appointed limits keep:

O hear us when we cry to Thee

For those in peril on the sea . . .

Music had made the moment.

Vera Lynn's sentimental performance of "White Cliffs of Dover" captured the emotional currents of war.

Matters were settled four months later with the Japanese attack on Pearl Harbor. At about five o'clock on the seemingly endless afternoon of Sunday, December 7, 1941—word of the Japanese strike had come a few hours earlier—President Roosevelt was preparing the war speech he was to deliver to Congress the next day. Summoning his secretary, Grace Tully, into his study, where he was seated at his desk, Roosevelt lit a cigarette, inhaled deeply, and went to work.

"Sit down, Grace," the president said. "I'm going before Congress tomorrow. I'd like to dictate my message. It will be short."

Roosevelt began, Tully recalled, with "the same calm tone in which he dictated his mail. Only his diction was a little different as he spoke each word incisively and slowly, carefully specifying each punctuation mark and paragraph. 'Yesterday comma December 7 comma 1941 dash a day which will live in world history dash the United States of America was suddenly and deliberately attacked by naval and air forces of the Empire of Japan period paragraph.'"

The address, as promised, was brief. "I ask," FDR dictated, "that the Congress declare that since the unprovoked and dastardly attack by Japan on Sunday comma December 7 comma a state of war has existed between the United States and the Japanese Empire period end." The president made a final edit, changing his initial phrase "world history" into the more memorable "infamy."

Roosevelt and Churchill met secretly at sea off Newfoundland in August 1941. At a shipboard church service, they sang hymns and prayed together. "It was," Churchill recalled, "a great hour to live."

THE WHITE CLIFFS OF DOVER and YOU'LL NEVER KNOW

"The White Cliffs of Dover" is incredibly pensive. Listening to Vera Lynn's version of this classic song, I am transported into her dream of what the future will bring. So wistful, it leaves any listener longing for the dark days to be over. And while I'm not sure Dover really *had* bluebirds, I can see how the song would capture the sentiment and imagination of the citizens of Britain and those who fought so valiantly in their skies.

"You'll Never Know" also resonated with the troops during World War II, and it's easy to see why. It was a hit in America with one of my idols, Frank Sinatra. Vera Lynn made it a hit in Britain. Her version embodies that feeling of separation for a soldier gone off to war—the longing, almost desperate tone in her delivery hits you straight in the heart. The track is sparse, letting the vocal stand out. She has placed herself within this song in a way that makes the listener not only believe everything she's saying but think that she's saying it straight to them. Performances like this are rare and should be treasured. It's an art to match songs with artists—and when it's done right, the result can be timeless.

—T.M.

The most moving music of the war was the music that moved the troops themselves—songs of longing and loss, of love and hope. There was "We'll Meet Again," "You'll Never Know," and big band numbers by Glenn Miller, Benny Goodman, and others. It was the age of songs such as "Boogie Woogie Bugle Boy," and Miller and the Andrews Sisters each had a hit with "Don't Sit Under the Apple Tree (with Anyone Else but Me)." Miller, whose "Moonlight Serenade" was a signature song, lobbied to join the military once America entered the war. (Born in 1904, he was in his late thirties.) Bing Crosby wrote the government a letter of recommendation, saying that Miller was "a very high type young man, full of resourcefulness, adequately intelligent and a suitable type to command men or assist in organization." Commissioned in the Army Air Force, Miller set out, he said, to "put a little more spring into the feet of our marching men and a little more joy into their hearts." Regular military bands resisted Miller's attempts to bring the music forward from the Great War to the 1940s. "Look, Captain Miller," one is said to have complained, "we played those Sousa marches straight in the last war and we did all right, didn't we?"

Sung from the perspective of a soldier at war, "We'll Meet Again" offered hope amid the gloom of separation.

"You certainly did, Major," Miller replied, according to the story. "But tell me one thing: Are you still flying the same planes you flew in the last war, too?"

Miller's mission to update military music beyond John Philip Sousa, author of such standards as "Stars and Stripes Forever," "Semper Fidelis" (the official Marine march), and "The Washington Post March," provoked a wartime controversy after *Time* quoted Miller saying, "There hasn't been a successful Army band in the country. . . . We've got to keep pace with the soldiers. . . . Why, there's no question about it—anybody can improve on Sousa." Miller denied making the remark, but the damage was done.

Yet Miller pressed on, playing for the troops, for war bond drives, and over the radio. On a broadcast on Saturday, June 10, 1944, a few days after D-Day, he announced, "It's been a big week for our side. Over on the beaches of Normandy our boys have fired the opening guns of the long awaited drive to liberate the world." The band's opener that day was "Flying Home," a jazz number by Lionel Hampton (Ella Fitzgerald would later sing a powerful version) that, for African American GIs, signified a journey toward the kind of freedom at home they'd been fighting for abroad.

Franklin Roosevelt died of a cerebral hemorrhage on the afternoon of Thursday, April 12, 1945, in his cottage at Warm Springs, Georgia. As the president's body was being moved to the train for the trip to Washington, a naval chief petty officer, Graham Jackson, tears streaming down his face, played "Going Home" on his accordion.

With that, Franklin Delano Roosevelt was taken north toward home—first to Washington and then to Hyde Park, New York, where he was buried in the rose garden at Springwood, his ancestral home on the banks of the Hudson. At Warm Springs, after "Going Home," Graham Jackson had played one of Roosevelt's favorite hymns, "Nearer, My God, to Thee." Its final verse:

> There in my Father's home, safe and at rest,
> There in my Savior's love, perfectly blest;
> Age after age to be nearer, my God, to Thee.

When President Reagan, in 1982, spoke of FDR's centennial, the language was eloquent: "Historians still debate the details of his intentions, his policies and their impact," Reagan said of Roosevelt. "But all agree that, like the Founding Fathers before him, FDR was an American giant, a leader who shaped, inspired, and led our people through perilous times. He meant many different things to many different people. He could reach out to men and women of diverse races and backgrounds and inspire them with new hope and new confidence in war and peace."

In the song "Tell Me Why You Like Roosevelt," Otis Jackson sang the same sentiments:

> In the year of nineteen and forty-five,
> A good president laid down and died.
> I knew how all the poor people felt,
> When they received the message "We've lost Roosevelt."

Woody Guthrie may have offered the most timeless memorial to the fallen Roosevelt. In a song addressed to Eleanor, Guthrie remembered FDR as a providential figure:

> Dear Mrs. Roosevelt, don't hang your head and cry;
> His mortal clay is laid away, but his good work fills the sky;
> This world was lucky to see him born.

There is, really, nothing more to say on the matter. The world *was* lucky to see him born.

CHAPTER SIX

WE SHALL OVERCOME

Bobby Dylan says what a lot of people my age feel, but cannot say.

—JOAN BAEZ

Lord have mercy on this land of mine.

—NINA SIMONE, in "Mississippi Goddam," written after the bombing of Birmingham's 16th Street Baptist Church, 1963

In a sense, songs are the *soul* of a movement.

—MARTIN LUTHER KING, JR.

In the early-evening hours of Monday, October 22, 1962—the speech was broadcast on television and on radio at 7:00 P.M. in the East—President John F. Kennedy solemnly warned the nation of an existential crisis: The Soviet Union was deploying missiles in Communist Cuba, an act that put enemy nuclear weapons less than fifteen minutes away from Washington, D.C.

The end of everything seemed all too possible. A year earlier, Robert Shelton of the *New York Times* had reviewed a Greenwich Village performance by a young folk singer, Bob Dylan. "His clothes may need a bit of tailoring," Shelton wrote of Dylan, "but when he works his guitar, harmonica or piano, and composes new songs faster than he can remember them, there is no doubt that he is bursting

A commemorative portfolio of the Wednesday, August 28, 1963, March on Washington, published by the National Urban League.

at the seams with talent." In the fall of 1962, Dylan had sat down at a typewriter and written the apocalyptic "A Hard Rain's A-Gonna Fall." It was, Dylan said, a "song of desperation . . . a song of terror." A biographer, Howard Sounes, wrote, "As the missile crisis reached its apogee in October, musicians all over Greenwich Village were playing the new song, including Richie Havens and Pete Seeger."

Born Robert Zimmerman in 1941 in Duluth, Minnesota, Dylan grew up in Hibbing—which he later described as a "town that was dying"—and legally changed his name in tribute to Dylan Thomas in 1962. Dylan liked to say that he'd wandered the country as a young man, once writing, "I was making my own [D]epression / I rode freight trains for kicks / An' got beat up for laughs / Cut grass for quarters / An' sang for dimes." In Greenwich Village and on the folk circuit, Dylan broke out, and his canon includes "The Death of Emmett Till," about the 1955 lynching of a Black teenager in Money, Mississippi; "The Times They Are A-Changin'"; "With God on Our Side"; and many others. "Bobby Dylan says what a lot of people my age feel, but cannot say," Joan Baez remarked in the first half of the decade. In the second half, the *Village Voice* critic Richard Goldstein wrote, "Today, he is Shakespeare and Judy Garland to my generation. We trust what he tells us."

Should total nuclear war come in the fall of 1962, though, there would be nothing left to tell: Singer and audience would be annihilated. It was just possible, then, that "A Hard Rain's A-Gonna Fall" would be the last song Dylan would ever write.

But in Washington, the president delivered.

History guided him hour by hour. In September 1960, Kennedy had written a review of a book by the British historian and strategist B. H. Liddell Hart, *Deterrent or Defense,* and highlighted this observation of Hart's: "Keep strong, if possible. In any case, keep cool. Have unlimited patience. Never corner an opponent, and always assist him to save face. Put yourself in his shoes—so as to see things through his eyes. Avoid self-righteousness like the devil—nothing is so self-blinding."

During those thirteen days, Kennedy considered things from the point of view of the Soviet premier, Nikita Khrushchev, and resisted rushing to judgment.

To JFK, history taught that pride, emotion, and hurry were the enemies of the good. "If anybody is around to write after this, they are going to understand that we made every effort to find peace and every effort to give our adversary room to move," JFK said at the time. "I am not going to push the Russians an inch beyond what is necessary." Reason trumped passion, and a deal—the removal of missiles in Cuba in exchange for the removal of missiles in Turkey—ended the crisis peaceably.

It was a glorious hour for diplomacy, for Dylan's "hard rain" had not fallen. "Even so," Howard Sounes wrote in his biography of Dylan, *Down the Highway,* "there was still a crackling energy in the air. Bob was the artist who had captured the zeitgeist in song, and he would do so again and again as the decade unraveled."

And unravel it did. In June 1963 in Tuscaloosa, Alabama, Governor George C. Wallace—who'd promised in his January inaugural to defend "segregation now . . . segregation tomorrow . . . segregation forever"—would fight the integration of the University of Alabama. In Mississippi, meanwhile, Medgar Evers, field secretary for the NAACP, would walk from his car to the door of his house in Jackson, and a shot would ring out. The *New York Times*'s Claude Sitton described the assassination: "The sniper's bullet struck him just below the right shoulder blade. The slug crashed through a front window of the home, penetrated an interior wall, ricocheted off a refrigerator and struck a coffee pot. . . . Evers staggered to the doorway, his keys in his hand, and collapsed near the steps. His wife, Myrlie, and their three children rushed to the door. . . .” The assassin was a Klansman, Byron De La Beckwith, and in response Bob Dylan wrote “Only a Pawn in Their Game,” a reflection on how white Southern politicians used race to keep poor whites consumed with hating Blacks—“to hang and to lynch.” And in September four little girls would die in a Klan bombing of the 16th Street Baptist Church in Birmingham.

The civil rights movement was powered by song. “The fear down here is tremendous,” said Phyllis Martin, field secretary for the Student Nonviolent Coordinating Committee (SNCC). “I didn’t know whether I’d be shot at, or stoned, or what. But when the singing started, I forgot all that. I felt good within myself. We sang ‘Oh Freedom’ and ‘We Shall Not Be Moved,’ and after that you just don’t want to sit around anymore. You want the world to hear you, to know what you’re fighting for!” To John Lewis, music was everything. “If it hadn’t been for music, the civil rights movement would have been like a bird without wings,” Lewis recalled. “I really believe that.”

Songs could put the white forces of oppression on notice. Bernice Johnson Reagon recalled a moment in Dawson, Georgia: “I sat in a church and felt the chill that ran through a small gathering of Blacks when the sheriff and his deputies walked in. They stood at the door, making sure everyone knew they were there. Then a song began. And the song made sure that the sheriff and his deputies knew we were there. We became visible, our image was enlarged, when the sound of the freedom songs filled all the space in that church.”

Music, then, could be a tool of justice. “In a sense, songs are the *soul* of a movement,” Martin Luther King, Jr., had observed in a *Playboy* interview published in January 1965. “Consider, in World War II, *‘Praise the Lord and Pass the Ammunition,’* and in World War I, *‘Over There’* . . . and during the Civil War, *‘Battle Hymn of the Republic’* and *‘John Brown’s Body.’* A Negro song anthology would include sorrow songs, shouts for joy, battle hymns, anthems. Since slavery, the Negro has sung throughout his struggle in America. '*Steal Away*' and '*Go Down, Moses*' were the songs of faith and inspiration which were sung on the plantations. For the same reasons the slaves sang, Negroes today sing freedom songs, for we, too, are in bondage. We sing out our determination that 'We shall overcome, black and white together, we shall overcome someday.'"

The lyrics King chose to underscore—"We Shall Overcome"—were from the anthem of the movement:

> We shall overcome, we shall overcome,
> We shall overcome someday;
> Oh, deep in my heart, I do believe,
> We shall overcome someday.

WE SHALL OVERCOME and I HAVE A DREAM

When I hear "We Shall Overcome," I think of Dr. Martin Luther King, Jr. I think most of us do.

And I sense the power of music to move people. The brilliance of "We Shall Overcome" lies in its capacity for many different voices to join in— a fitting metaphor if ever there was one. A folk song, it has all the hallmarks of great folk music in that it summons the listeners to become singers—it's music as action.

With Dr. King's "I Have a Dream"—not a song, but a kind of prose poetry— I hear the passion from *all* of Dr. King's sermons. I have recollections of seeing clips of Dr. King's speech at the March on Washington from very early on in my life. Indeed, this speech deeply touched me and made me realize for the first time the strength in words delivered masterfully. Politicians, preachers, and singers are really in the same business—using sound to move hearts and change minds. More than half a century after his assassination in Memphis, Dr. King sings still. —T.M.

As much hymn as ballad, "We Shall Overcome" has a kind of stateliness, a certain dignity. "It made us feel we could face almost anything—the storms of the movement, the storms of life itself," John Lewis recalled. "Nobody could turn us around." Lewis's memories of the movement are set to music. When he thinks of Mississippi, he remembers sitting in a field in Greenwood with "Bobby Dylan—he was singing, quietly, for us." And when he thinks of Alabama, he recalls the lyrics he and his fellow SNCC volunteers would make up on the spot:

> Oh, Wallace, you can never jail us all
> Segregation's gonna fall.

They'd sing these improvised words with conviction, for they knew that no matter how tortuous the path to justice, justice was in fact on their side.

Dylan's work in particular helped spark other artists. After "Blowin' in the Wind," for example, Sam Cooke wrote "A Change Is Gonna Come." A son of the Mississippi Delta, Cooke was a gospel singer—he first came to prominence with the group the Soul Stirrers—who made a pioneering professional shift into popular music and was a successful music-business entrepreneur. His hits included "You Send Me," "Chain Gang," and "Twisting the Night Away"; the Rock & Roll Hall of Fame—Cooke was inducted, posthumously, in 1986—describes him as "the definitive soul man . . . seductive, devoted, elegant, and moving. These qualities, combined with his dazzling, pure voice, made him irresistible to audiences regardless of race or religion."

"A Change Is Gonna Come," released in late 1964, is Cooke's most political song. Reflecting on the song's fiftieth anniversary, the music writer David Cantwell argued in a *New Yorker* essay that Cooke and Dylan "were wading up different streams of the American song for inspiration. Dylan found much of his melody in the nineteenth-century Black spiritual 'No More Auction Block for Me' . . . , while his voice and phrasing, and his austere and static strum, are indebted to the Depression-era folk style of Woody Guthrie. By contrast, the melody to 'A Change Is Gonna Come,' with its

The Rock & Roll Hall of Fame calls Sam Cooke "the definitive soul man."

long dynamic lines that trek the peaks and valleys of arranger Rene Hall's lush orchestral landscape, shows Cooke working off of Tin Pan Alley standards, film music, and show tunes." Cantwell believed that Cooke was drawing in part on "Ol' Man River," the number from Jerome Kern and Oscar Hammerstein's 1927 musical *Show Boat,* a song generally associated with Paul Robeson. "A Change Is Gonna Come," Cantwell wrote, was a formidable thing: "brooding but bright."

Ray Charles had recently (in 1963) recorded his own cover of "Ol' Man River," and Chuck Berry had released "Promised Land" in 1964, a rock-and-roll number describing a cross-country journey from Norfolk, Virginia, through the segregated South to a new day in California. Berry wasn't known to be political, which makes "Promised Land" a sign of how pervasive the civil rights movement had become and how the convention of "masking" (the conveyance of political meaning in religious or, sometimes, in seemingly innocuous terms) continued to be essential. Berry was singing about the route of the Freedom Rides—the bus trips that white and Black activists took part in throughout the American South in 1961 to protest segregated bus terminals—but he never said so directly, thus making the song playable on the radio.

A CHANGE IS GONNA COME

Two things strike me about Sam Cooke and this song. First is his nature as a true artist. At the top of his game, he took a huge creative risk with "A Change Is Gonna Come." Born in Mississippi but raised in Chicago, Sam Cooke experienced the horrors of the Jim Crow South firsthand while touring. He saw folk artists like Dylan writing clever protest songs and knew that he had an even larger platform through his success in pop music. (He was ahead of his time in business, too, having started his own publishing company and record label.) Sam could be heard by both Black and white audiences at once and deliver an individual message to both. There's a pain in his voice as he addresses the issue of segregation, and yet a strength that he's certain things will get better ("I *know* a change is gonna come") at a time when he couldn't really be so certain.

Second was his artistic bravery. As a musician with hits, there's always pressure to keep doing what you've done. I am grateful—and inspired—that Sam Cooke didn't do that. He was brave. He wrote a song of truth and hope at a time when being careful and putting out another "Twist" would have been easier and far less risky.   —T.M.

Curtis Mayfield of the Impressions was a master of masking. Reflecting on his "Keep On Pushing," a song about the determination to press on against all odds and all obstacles, Mayfield observed, "Gospel was your foundation and there's been many a song coming from the black church. All you had to do was change some few lyrics. 'Keep On Pushing' was intended, written[,] as a gospel song. But all I needed to do to lock it in with the Impressions was say 'I've got my strength' instead of 'God gave me strength.'" Other examples of songs heard very differently by white and Black audiences include Ray Charles's "Georgia On My Mind," which he recorded in 1960; Stevie Wonder's "I Was Made to Love Her"; Martha Reeves's "Dancing in the Street"; and Ruby and the Romantics' "Our Day Will Come."

Chuck Berry's apparently apolitical hit "Johnny B. Goode" fell into this category, too. In his autobiography, Berry expressed pride that the song is the story of talent, perseverance, and success. "I imagine most black people naturally realize but I feel safe in stat-

"If they ask you who you are," Odetta said at the march, "tell them you're a child of God."

ing that NO white person can conceive of the feeling of obtaining Caucasian respect in the wake of a world of dark denial, simply because it is impossible to view the dark side when faced with brilliance," Berry wrote. "'Johnny B. Goode' was created as all other things and brought out of a modern dark age. With encouragement he chose to practice, shading himself along the roadside but seen by the brilliance of his guitar playing. Chances are you have talent. But will the name and the light come to you? No! You have to 'Go!'"

Joan Baez, Bob Dylan, and Peter, Paul, and Mary performed at the March on Washington.

At the March on Washington for Jobs and Freedom on Wednesday, August 28, 1963, Joan Baez sang "We Shall Overcome" to the crowd on the National Mall; she was one of fourteen performers who were an official part of the day of speeches and solemnities. The songs of the March on Washington offer a microcosm of the political panoply of life in these years as gospel and folk, and Black and white, came together to acknowledge the difficulty of the struggle and the justice of the claims of those seeking equality.

The marchers themselves sang en route to and on the mall. From the microphone, Odetta cried out, "If they ask you who you are, tell them you're a child of God," and sang "I'm On My Way." Dylan sang "Only a Pawn in Their Game" (unimpressed, Russell Baker of the *Times* called it "a lugubrious mountain song") and, with Baez, "When the Ship Comes In," which struck a deliverance theme.

Peter, Paul, and Mary performed "If I Had a Hammer" and Dylan's "Blowin' in the Wind," which they'd already recorded and released on Tuesday, June 18, 1963. A huge hit, their rendition of "Blowin' in the Wind" was reported to be "the fastest-selling single in the history of Warner Records," and it was resonating culturally and politically. "Radio stations in Cleveland, Washington, Philadelphia, and Worcester, Mass., have played 'Blowin' in the Wind' every hour on the hour," the *New York Times* reported, "some as a pop tune and others as a broadcast 'editorial.'" The Freedom Singers were there, and Mahalia Jackson sang two gospel songs—"I Been 'Buked and I Been Scorned" and "How I Got Over."

Jackson did more than sing. When Martin Luther King stepped to the microphones for his remarks, he did not begin as well as he'd hoped. His sermon had been drafted by too many hands late the previous night at the Willard Hotel, and

Mahalia Jackson sang "I Been 'Buked and I Been Scorned" and "How I Got Over"; she also prompted King, as she put it, to "Tell 'em about the dream."

one sentence he was about to deliver was particularly awkward: "And so today, let us go back to our communities as members of the international association for the advancement of creative dissatisfaction."

He'd begun to extemporize, searching for the right words to stir the crowd, when Jackson, who was standing nearby, spoke up. "Tell 'em about the dream, Martin," Jackson said. King left his text altogether at this point. "I have a dream," King continued, "that one day this nation will rise up, live out the true meaning of its creed: 'We hold these truths to be self-evident, that all men are created equal.'"

Drawing on "My Country, 'Tis of Thee," King projected an ideal vision of an exceptional nation:

> I have a dream today. . . .
>
> I have a dream that one day every valley shall be exalted, every hill and mountain shall be made low, the rough places will be made plain, and the crooked places will be made straight, and the glory of the Lord shall be revealed, and all flesh shall see it together.
>
> This is our hope. This is the faith that I go back to the South with. With this faith we will be able to hew out of the mountain of despair a stone of hope. With this faith we will be able to transform the jangling discords of our nation into a beautiful symphony of brotherhood. With this faith we will be able to work together, to pray together, to struggle together, to go to jail together, to stand up for freedom together, knowing that we will be free one day.
>
> This will be the day when all of God's children will be able to sing with new meaning: "My country, 'tis of thee, sweet land of liberty, of thee I sing. Land where my fathers died, land of the pilgrims' pride, from every mountainside, let freedom ring!'"

BLOWIN' IN THE WIND

If there ever was an answer that's hard to understand, it would be "the answer" that Bob Dylan tells us is "blowin' in the wind."

Maybe that's a huge piece of this masterpiece—the ambiguity. He leaves it up to us to figure out what it all means. Lord knows this can be frustrating, but some of the most powerful songs let you fill in the gaps, leaving intentional space in words or thoughts or unusual phrases that challenge the listener to think and reflect. There is huge power in that.   —T.M.

By closing with the words of Samuel Francis Smith, words composed 132 years before in Andover and once sung from these steps by Marian Anderson, words lifted countless times by countless Americans, words of freedom and of aspiration, King framed the civil rights cause as a fundamentally *American* cause.

By summoning the words of Samuel Francis Smith in "My Country, 'Tis of Thee" in his peroration, King framed the civil rights cause as a fundamentally American one.

Marian Anderson sang that day, thus linking her 1939 breakthrough moment with that of the present. She was offering, she told the crowd, a "Negro spiritual," "He's Got the Whole World in His Hands"—old words now being sung to bring about a new world.

The glow did not last. On Sunday morning, September 15, 1963, in Birmingham, Alabama—the third Sunday after the March on Washington—fourteen-year-old William Bell was getting ready for church when he heard the explosion. It was 10:22 A.M., and the sound of the dynamite going off at the 16th Street Baptist Church roared across the city. The noise startled the Bells, who lived nearly three miles away on Fifth Avenue Southwest, in the city's Titusville neighborhood. Young Bell's father rushed him and the rest of the family into the car and drove to the church, where they found chaos and tragedy. Four young girls, Bell's contemporaries, had been massacred when the dynamite hidden by a group of Ku Klux Klansmen went off: Denise McNair, age eleven, and Carole Robertson, Cynthia Wesley, and Addie Mae Collins, all fourteen. "Every individual in this town knew at least one of the girls or knew their families," Bell, who grew up to

Denise McNair, 11; Carole Robertson, 14; Addie Mae Collins, 14; and Cynthia Wesley, 14, were murdered in the Klan bombing of Birmingham's 16th Street Baptist Church on Sunday, September 15, 1963.

serve as Birmingham's mayor, recalled. "Carole Robertson is a cousin of mine. Denise McNair went to school with my brother. Her mother taught my brother. You felt it, the pain of it."

News of the attack reached a young musician, Nina Simone, as she sat on that Sunday morning in her garage-apartment hideaway in Mount Vernon, New York. Descended from enslaved Black Southerners, Simone had been born in Tryon, North Carolina, in 1933 and was making her mark in the New York world of soul music as the movement gathered momentum. She was friends with Langston Hughes and James Baldwin, but she acknowledged that her focus was largely on her career and her young family, not on civil rights. "I was always aware of what the vanguard of black artists and thinkers were concerned with," Simone re-called, "but I wasn't an activist in any sense; I heard the conversations flow around me at Langston's or in the Blue Note with Jimmy Baldwin . . . and a political awareness seeped into me without my having even to think about it. But I wasn't taking the trouble to educate myself in an organized way—where would I find the time?"

Then came the Evers assassination and the 16th Street church bombing. "It was more than I could take, and I sat struck dumb in my den like St. Paul on the road to Damascus,"

"It was more than I could take," Nina Simone said of the news of the attack on the 16th Street Baptist Church, "and I sat struck dumb in my den like St. Paul on the road to Damascus."

Simone recalled. "I suddenly realized what it was to be black in America in 1963, but it wasn't an intellectual connection . . . it came as a rush of fury, hatred, and determination."

Within an hour, Simone, sitting at her piano, had composed what she called her "first civil rights song, and it erupted out of me quicker than I could write it down." It was called "Mississippi Goddam." In performance, she would say, "The name of this tune is 'Mississippi Goddam,' and I mean every word of it":

The resulting song, "Mississippi Goddam," was recorded live at Carnegie Hall and released in 1964.

> Alabama's gotten me so upset
> Tennessee made me lose my rest
> And everybody knows about Mississippi
>   goddam
> Alabama's gotten me so upset
> Tennessee made me lose my rest
> And everybody knows about Mississippi goddam
> Can't you see it
> Can't you feel it
> It's all in the air
> I can't stand the pressure much longer
> Somebody say a prayer
> Alabama's gotten me so upset
> Tennessee made me lose my rest
> And everybody knows about Mississippi goddam . . .
> Hound dogs on my trail
> School children sitting in jail

Black cat cross my path
I think every day's gonna be my last
Lord have mercy on this land of mine
We all gonna get it in due time
I don't belong here
I don't belong there
I've even stopped believing in prayer

So much was happening so fast; so much blood was being shed. Hearing the news of the Birmingham church bombing on the radio, John Lewis, a young activist with the Student Nonviolent Coordinating Committee, traveled to Birmingham from his parents' home in Pike County, Alabama. Late in the afternoon of the day of the attack, he was there, outside the sanctuary, wondering. "It was unreal to stand there and try to absorb what had happened," Lewis recalled. "I looked at the people standing on that sidewalk across the street, these black men and women of Birmingham, who had lived through so much, and I knew that they had to be asking themselves, How much *more*? What *else*? What's *next*? . . . Four children killed on a Sunday morning in church, in God's house. What *could* be next?"

MISSISSIPPI GODDAM

This song was banned by certain radio stations, and it's a hard song to listen to. But we have to listen to it, because art is about truth—and Nina Simone was speaking the rawest kind of truth.

Nina Simone wrote it in a dark moment. Medgar Evers, the NAACP field secretary in Mississippi, had been shot down outside his house; four little girls had been murdered inside Birmingham's 16th Street Baptist Church in a terrorist attack planned and executed by Ku Klux Klansmen.

> Simone used to say that her art was a reflection of her times.
>
> That's what hits me here. This song practically requires you to look within, regardless of how painful that might be, and acknowledge the truth so that you can find the path forward. —T.M.

King preached the funeral for three of the four victims. "God still has a way of wringing good out of evil," he said. "And history has proven over and over again that unmerited suffering is redemptive. The innocent blood of these little girls may well serve as a redemptive force that will bring new light to this dark city."

John Coltrane's jazz composition "Alabama" took its cadences from King's eulogy. In this Coltrane was working in a tradition of "socially aware jazz" that included Art Blakey's "Freedom Rider," Max Roach's "Freedom Now Suite," and Charles Mingus's "Fables for Faubus."

In the streets outside the funeral services, mourners sang improvised verses to the tune of "We Shall Overcome":

> They did not die in vain.
> They did not die in vain,
> We shall overcome
> Someday.

In October 1963, President Kennedy contemplated the connection between the artistic and political worlds on a trip to Amherst College. The small liberal-arts college in Massachusetts was breaking ground for a library that would be named for the late Robert Frost. An admirer of Frost's who had arranged for the poet to read at his inauguration in 1961, President Kennedy was happy to speak at the ceremony.

At Amherst, Kennedy talked of the place he had come to. "Many years ago, Woodrow Wilson said, what good is a political party unless it's serving a great national purpose?" the president asked. "And what good is a private college or university unless it's serving a great national purpose?" He reminded his listeners that their luck in life came at a price: service to others. JFK paraphrased Winston Churchill, who had said, at Harvard University in 1943, "The price of greatness is responsibility." Kennedy made the point this way: "Privilege is here, and with privilege goes responsibility."

To JFK, protest was part and parcel of the project of America. "If sometimes our great artists have been the most critical of our society, it is because their sensitivity and their concern for justice, which must motivate any true artist, makes him aware that our Nation falls short of its highest potential," the president said. "I see little of more importance to the future of our country and our civilization than full recognition of the place of the artist." To Kennedy, "the highest duty of the writer, the composer, the artist is to remain true to himself and to let the chips fall where they may. In serving his vision of the truth, the artist best serves his nation."

Kennedy led practically, and he led spiritually. We can ask for no more than that.

Then came Dallas. Assassinated on Friday, November 22, 1963, Kennedy was buried at Arlington National Cemetery after rites at the Capitol and a funeral mass at St. Matthew's Cathedral. Washington, it was said, was filled with the sounds of sobs and with the music of the Navy hymn, "Eternal Father, Strong to Save," played in honor of Kennedy's service in the Pacific in World War II. Its final verse:

O Trinity of love and power!
Our brethren shield in danger's hour;

From rock and tempest, fire and foe.
Protect them wheresoever they go. . . .

On Sunday, March 7, 1965, a voting-rights march from Selma to Montgomery had barely begun when Alabama state troopers charged a line of nonviolent demonstrators led by the twenty-five-year-old John Lewis. Inhaling tear gas and reeling from two billy-club blows to his head, Lewis felt everything dimming. He could hear screams and slurs and the clop-clop-clop of the troopers' horses. His skull fractured, his vision blurred, Lewis believed the end had come. "People are going to die here," he said to himself. "*I'm* going to die here."

Television cameras recorded the Alabama troopers' attack on Lewis and his fellow marchers. That evening, ABC interrupted a Sunday night broadcast of the film *Judgment at Nuremberg* to show the footage. The day would come to be known as "Bloody Sunday," and the scene at the bridge proved a turning point in the life of the nation.

The day's violence inspired music such as Grant Green's "The Selma March," from the album *His Majesty King Funk,* but the larger legacy came in a more traditional setting: that of a presidential address.

At two minutes past nine o'clock on the evening of Monday, March 15, President Lyndon Johnson addressed the Congress and seventy million Americans. "At times history and fate meet at a single time in a single place to shape a turning point in man's unending search for freedom. So it was at Lexington and Concord. So it was a century ago at Appomattox. So it was last week in Selma, Alabama." Johnson continued:

This was the first nation in the history of the world to be founded with a purpose. The great phrases of that purpose still sound in

"People are going to die here," said John Lewis, shown here under attack on Bloody Sunday in Selma. "*I'm* going to die here."

every American heart, North and South: "All men are created equal"—"government by consent of the governed"—"give me liberty or give me death." Well, those are not just clever words, or those are not just empty theories. In their name Americans have fought and died for two centuries, and tonight around the world they stand there as guardians of our liberty, risking their lives. . . . Many of the issues of civil rights are very complex and most difficult. But about this there can and should be no argument. Every American citizen must have an equal right to vote. There is no reason which can excuse the denial of that right. There is no duty which weighs more heavily on us than the duty we have to ensure that right.

King and Lewis wept as they watched President Johnson invoke the mantra of the movement: "And we shall overcome."

Yet the harsh fact is that in many places in this country men and women are kept from voting simply because they are Negroes. . . .

There is no moral issue. It is wrong—deadly wrong—to deny any of your fellow Americans the right to vote in this country.

There is no issue of States rights or national rights. There is only the struggle for human rights. . . .

What happened in Selma is part of a far larger movement which reaches into every section and State of America. It is the effort of American Negroes to secure for themselves the full blessings of American life.

Their cause must be our cause too. Because it is not just Negroes, but really it is all of us, who must overcome the crippling legacy of bigotry and injustice.

And we shall overcome.

And we shall overcome. As he listened to Johnson repeat the civil rights refrain, King, watching in Selma, wept. The song of a movement had become the mantra of a president.

King's and Lewis's nonviolent strategy was hardly the only vision on offer in the war to change the calculus of race and power in America. Malcolm X and the Black Power Movement wanted to move further, faster—"by any means necessary," in Malcolm's words. In a January 1965 telegram he sent to George Lincoln Rockwell, the head of the American Nazi Party, Malcolm warned that if Rockwell's "present racist agitation against our people there in Alabama causes physical harm to Reverend King or any other black Americans who are only attempting to enjoy their rights as free human beings . . . you and your Ku Klux Klan friends will be met with maximum physical retaliation from those of us who are not handcuffed by the disarming philosophy of nonviolence, and who believe in asserting our right of self-defense—by any means necessary."

Malcolm loved music and understood its innate power. "Music, Brother, is ours—it is us—and like us it is always here—surrounding us—like the infinite particles that make up Life, it cannot be seen—but can only be felt—Like Life!!!" Malcolm wrote in a 1950 letter.

In 1967, Aretha Franklin took a song of Otis Redding's—"Respect"—and made it her own forever. "For the Black Panthers and their supporters, 'Respect' sent an unambiguous message to white America: From now on, black folk would take care of business in their own way," Craig Werner wrote in his *A Change Is Gonna Come: Music, Race, and the Soul of America.*

"Respect," in Franklin's hands, was not only an assertion of Black pride but also of gender. It was heard as a feminist anthem. "There is no one who can touch her," Mary J. Blige wrote of Franklin in *Rolling Stone.* "She is the reason why women want to sing." Franklin's rendition of Gerry Goffin and Carole King's "(You Make Me Feel Like) a Natural Woman" was another song that put a woman's experience at the center of the narrative. Of Franklin, Barack Obama told the *New Yorker*'s David Remnick in 2016, "Nobody embodies more fully the connection between the African-American spiritual, the blues, R&B, rock and roll—the way that hardship and sorrow were transformed into something full of beauty and vitality and hope. American history wells up when Aretha sings. That's why, when she sits down at a piano and sings 'A Natural Woman,' she can move me to tears."

The hour was late, about half past nine on the evening of Wednesday, April 3, 1968. At the Mason Temple in Memphis, the seat of the Pentecostal Church of God in Christ, Martin Luther King began to speak. A heavy storm had blown through at dusk, keeping turnout light at the rally for the city's striking sanitation workers.

"Well, I don't *know* what will happen now," King told the crowd. "We've got some difficult days ahead. But it really doesn't matter with me now. Because I've been to the mountaintop. And I don't mind." He went on:

> Like anybody, I would like to live—a long life—longevity has its place. But I'm not concerned about that now. I just want to do God's will.

And He's allowed me to go up to the mountain. And I've looked over. And I have seen the promised land. I may not get there with you. But I want you to *know, tonight,* that we, as a people, will get to the promised land!

Above the cries of his followers, many of whom were transported by the emotion of his presentation, King uttered his final public words: "Mine eyes have seen the glory of the coming of the Lord!"

And so there is a line, however jagged, between Julia Ward Howe, who hastily composed her hymn of liberty in the dark of night more than a century before, and the last earthly evening of Martin Luther King.

The next day—Thursday, April 4—King retreated to Room 306 at the Lorraine Motel, worrying about the strike and working on his sermon for Sunday. Its title: "Why America May Go to Hell." By 5:00 P.M., he was hungry and looked forward to supper. Always fastidious—a prince of the church—King shaved, put on cologne, and stepped onto the balcony. He paused; a .30-06 rifle shot slammed him back against the wall.

At King's funeral services in Atlanta, "My Heavenly Father, Watch Over Me" and "If I Can Help Somebody" were sung, and his old friend Mahalia Jackson took the stage at a public memorial at Morehouse College. She was, the *Washington Post* reported, "crying with anguish into the microphone" as she honored his last request. "Precious Lord," she sang, "take my hand / Lead me on, let me stand."

King's mortal pilgrimage was done. A distraught Nina Simone's "Why (The King of Love Is Dead)" paid tribute; in Atlanta, a mule-drawn cart carried his body through the city's streets. An estimated one hundred twenty million Americans watched the funeral. Mourners in the April heat included Jacqueline Kennedy, Richard Nixon, Robert F. Kennedy, Hubert H. Humphrey, Harry Belafonte,

Marlon Brando, Sammy Davis, Jr., Aretha Franklin, Eartha Kitt, Jackie Robinson, Diana Ross and the Supremes, and Stevie Wonder. The segregationist governor of Georgia, Lester Maddox, declined to attend, spending the day in the gold-domed state capitol under an increased guard. He was, *Newsweek* wrote, worried about "the expected onset of Armageddon." "If they come in here," Maddox told his troopers, "we're gonna stack 'em up." Yet there was no violence from the surging mourners in Atlanta—only grief.

The march to the cemetery was long—more than three and a half miles—

Coretta Scott King led the march of mourners behind the mule-drawn cart bearing her husband's body from Ebenezer Baptist Church. The silence was interrupted by choruses of "The Battle Hymn of the Republic" and "We Shall Overcome," among other songs of the movement.

and the silence was interrupted from time to time by choruses of "The Battle Hymn of the Republic," "We Shall Overcome," "This Little Light of Mine," and "Dr. King Comes Marching In," sung to the tune of "When the Saints Go Marching In."

At journey's end, King's epitaph was drawn not from scripture but from the canon of African American spirituals: "Free at last; free at last; thank God Almighty I'm free at last."

CHAPTER SEVEN

ARCHIE BUNKER VS. THE AGE OF AQUARIUS

> I want to thank you, Mr. President, not for any one thing, just for everything.
> —JOHN WAYNE, in remarks to Richard Nixon, 1973

> We gotta get out of this place.
> —THE ANIMALS, in a song popular with American troops in Southeast Asia

Richard Nixon was desperate for friendly faces. In the late winter of 1974, as the Watergate scandal (a break-in at the Democratic National Committee head-quarters that was linked back to Nixon) enveloped him and talk of impeachment grew more insistent, the besieged president flew from Washington to Nashville, the capital of a state, Tennessee, that he'd carried with 67.7 percent of the vote against George McGovern in 1972.

Arriving in Nashville on Saturday, March 16, Nixon held a rally at a Tennessee Air National Guard hangar, and the cheers of the crowd overwhelmed protest-ers who were chanting for impeachment. Leaving nothing to chance, the White House had sent technicians to town five days earlier to make sure the sound sys-tem was optimal for the president's remarks. One 1969 country song, by Merle

In a surreal White House meeting, Elvis Presley called on
President Nixon on Monday, December 21, 1970.

Seeking a friendly venue as Watergate engulfed him, Nixon spent an evening at the Grand Ole Opry in March 1974.

Haggard, had become a kind of Middle American anthem, "Okie from Muskogee."

Through the years Haggard could be ambivalent about "Okie." "We wrote it to be satirical originally," Haggard recalled. "But then people latched on to it, and it really turned into this song that looked into the mindset of people [the hippies] so opposite of who and where we were." A Reuters piece in 1970 observed that "Haggard has tapped, perhaps for the first time in popular music, a vast reservoir of resentment among Americans against the long-haired young and their 'underground' society." In a 1970 *Rolling Stone* interview, Haggard was blunt about the counterculture protestors: "I don't like their views on life, their filth, their visible self-disrespect." In later years he said that he'd been "dumb as a rock" when he wrote the song, but at other times he could also stand by it. "That's how I got into it with the hippies," he said on another occasion. "I thought they were unqualified to judge America, and I thought about them lookin' down their noses at something that I cherished very much, and it pissed me off."

Whatever Haggard's views about the song—then or later—it was popular in Nixon's America (as was Haggard's "The Fightin' Side of Me," another hit from 1969). In Nashville, supporters of the president passed out song sheets entitled "Stand Up and Cheer for Richard Nixon," sung to the tune of "Okie from Muskogee":

> I'm sick of what I'm reading in the papers,
> I'm tired of all that trash on TV,
> Stand up and cheer for Richard Nixon . . .
> I've been hearing talk about impeaching
> The man we chose to lead us through these
>   times.
> But talk like this could weaken and defeat
>   us,
> Let's show the world we're not the quitting kind.

In "Okie from Muskogee," Merle Haggard gave the "silent majority" a song to sing.

Onstage with Roy Acuff later in the evening, Nixon turned to the business at hand. Returning POWs from Vietnam, the president said, thrilled to country music more than to any other genre—"it touched them and touched them deeply after that long time away from America." He went on:

> What country music is, is that first it comes from the heart of
> America, because this is the heart of America, out here in Middle
> America. Second, it relates to those experiences that mean so much
> to America. It talks about family, it talks about religion, the faith
> in God that is so important to our country and particularly to our

family life. And as we all know, country music radiates a love of this Nation, [of] patriotism.

Country music, therefore, has those combinations which are so essential to America's character at a time that America needs character, because today—one serious note—let me tell you, the peace of the world for generations, maybe centuries to come, will depend not just on America's military might, which is the greatest in the world, or our wealth, which is the greatest in the world, but it is going to depend on our character, our belief in ourselves, our love of country, our willingness to not only wear the flag but to stand up for the flag. And country music does that.

Nixon knew his audience. The South was both hospitable and hawkish, an unusual combination in the years of LBJ and of Nixon. As the war in Vietnam unfolded, claiming about fifty-eight thousand American lives, followed by Watergate and Nixon's fall, America was at once in conflict and in conversation with itself. The country was riven by region, class, party, and religion; America seemed best understood as a struggle at home between the musical *Hair*'s Age of Aquarius and Archie Bunker, the fictional protagonist of Norman Lear's television series *All in the Family.*

We can hear the sounds of that battle in the music of the era. Social customs and values largely taken for granted were under assault. The country seemed powerless in Vietnam and unmoored at home. By late 1967, columnist Joseph Kraft had put the phrase "Middle Americans" in political circulation. Nixon called them "the great silent majority."

From Woodstock to the marches for peace in Washington, the great antiwar music and the countercultural touchstones loom large even now. John Lennon's call to "Give Peace a Chance" has a more dominant place in the popular memory than, say, Loretta Lynn's "Dear Uncle Sam" or John Wayne's recording of John Mitchum's prose poem to the nation of Richard Nixon, "America, Why I Love Her." Yet an understanding of the America of that tumultuous time—and an understanding of the first decades of the twenty-first century—requires an appreciation of the tensions and divergent views of the United States in the Vietnam era.

★★

OKIE FROM MUSKOGEE and THE AGE OF AQUARIUS

Pivoting off the counterculture, Merle Haggard composed and recorded the country music standard "Okie from Muskogee." In just six weeks, "Okie" would top the country singles chart and go on to win single of the year from the Country Music Association.

Anything Haggard moves me. It's practically in my DNA. You could say I graduated from the college of Merle. Probably no other individual country artist was a bigger influence on me. His stark lyrics, delivered with the ultimate country voice, move the listener.

Preceding "Okie from Muskogee" by six months is "The Age of Aquarius." "Aquarius/Let the Sunshine In" was a big hit single for the 5th Dimension, who released "Aquarius" together with the title "Let the Sunshine In" as a medley from the musical *Hair*. *Billboard* magazine ranked it as the number two single for the year 1969. Although it came at the end of the decade, this song came to define the end of the sixties and the hippie movement.

I would come to discover the medley years later. Are they songs of protest? To me, they are songs of change—they are among those songs that bridge the gap of generational change.   —T.M.

Staff Sergeant Barry Sadler, a member of the army's elite special forces, sang "The Ballad of the Green Berets," written by Sadler and Robin Moore, on *The Ed Sullivan Show,* on Sunday, January 30, 1966. (John Wayne would star in a 1969 movie, *The Green Berets,* that also helped popularize the song.) Standing ramrod straight, in uniform, before an image of the Green Beret insignia bearing the Latin motto *De Oppresso Liber* (To free the oppressed), Sadler, who'd been wounded in Vietnam, painted a portrait of valor and strength.

The war in Vietnam starkly divided the nation along political and cultural lines—chasms reflected in the music of the era.

In 1966, a song like "The Ballad of the Green Berets" could find a big audience. It was, in fact, "*the* most popular song of 1966," Doug Bradley and Craig

Werner wrote in *We Gotta Get Out of This Place: The Soundtrack of the Vietnam War,* "surpassing 'We Can Work It Out,' 'Paint It Black,' the Association's 'Cherish,' and a host of Motown classics, including the Four Tops' 'Reach Out, I'll Be There' and the Supremes' 'You Can't Hurry Love.'"

By 1968, however, with the draft, increasing troop deployments, the miseries of combat, and no clear path to victory, voices of protest rose in a crescendo. Sixty-eight was the nadir of virtually everything. "It was a year which dealt badly with everyone whom it touched," Ward Just wrote in the *Washington Post* toward the end of 1968. "It struck down the good and the bad indiscriminately, and at the end of it, by November, the country seemed no closer to healing the sickness—whatever it was. Querulous, dissatisfied, mad, the public looked for explanations; the public looked for leaders." The essay quoted Paul Simon and Art Garfunkel, and their quiet cri de coeur, "Mrs. Robinson," which longed for heroes, as representative of the angst of the age.

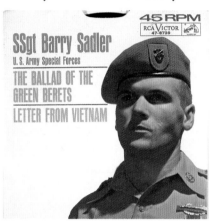

"The Ballad of the Green Berets" was the number one song in America in 1966.

Restoration and redemption would take more than Joe DiMaggio, who was name-checked in Simon and Garfunkel's hit. "I look over this campus, and I don't see many black faces," Robert Kennedy told students in Omaha during the intense RFK presidential campaign that ended when Kennedy was gunned down in the kitchen of the Ambassador Hotel in Los Angeles. "What you want is for the poor boy to fight this war, the boy whose parents haven't the money to send him to college . . . I don't think that's acceptable."

Creedence Clearwater Revival wrote a song, "Fortunate Son," which lamented what Kennedy had been talking about: the ability of the rich and the well connected to elude military service. The song was "a confrontation between me and Richard Nixon," CCR's John Fogerty recalled. "The haves, the people who have it all . . . During the Vietnam War, these were the people who didn't have to go to war. I was thinking about David Eisenhower, the grandson of Dwight, who married Julie Nixon."

★★★★★★★★★★★★★★★★★★★★★★★★★★★★★

THE BALLAD OF THE GREEN BERETS and FORTUNATE SON

"The Ballad of the Green Berets" is a great patriotic song.

It's hard not to feel pride when you listen to it. Maybe it's not cool to say that, but it's true: Barry Sadler's anthem is traditional in tone and in theme, and tradition works musically here.

Three years later brought a very different song. In 1969, Creedence Clearwater Revival released "Fortunate Son," a rock number incorporating the timeless motif of poor men fighting rich men's wars. (John Fogerty himself served in the Army Reserve.)

What I feel is the intensity of Fogerty's vocal delivery. Whereas Barry Sadler was matter-of-fact, angst and anger are the dominant emotions in CCR's song. Placed over a rock track—bass, drums, and electric guitars—there's no escaping the point of the powerful words, which are allowed to stand out.

"Fortunate Son" comes in at just over two minutes long. That was all CCR needed to create something that would be added to the National Recording Registry by the Library of Congress for its significance to the time.   —T.M.

Pete Seeger was even more direct in "Bring Them Home," and, in 1967, he'd released the antiwar "Waist Deep in the Big Muddy," which implicitly took on President Johnson's leadership. In the lyrics, Seeger evoked 1942 and a "big fool" of a commanding officer who insists, stupidly, that a platoon cross an un-crossable river—and the commander refuses to recognize reality no matter how bad things get. "It got the most explosive approval of any song I have ever sung," Seeger recalled, and CBS cut it from a taped appearance of Seeger on *The Smothers Brothers Comedy Hour* in 1967. (The network later caved and allowed the song to be broadcast; only the CBS affiliate in Detroit refused to air it altogether.)

Edwin Starr recorded the antiwar "War" in 1970, but other songs were more subtle. Jimmy Webb wrote "Galveston," sung by Glen Campbell, from the perspective of a soldier afraid and far from home.

Pete Seeger's "Waist Deep in the Big Muddy" and "Bring Them Home" were powerful antiwar anthems.

That was the view from the U.S. troops in Vietnam; Martha and the Vandellas reversed the perspective with their 1966 "Jimmy Mack." It's a complicated piece because it's as much about temptation as it is about steadfast loyalty in love—the last thing a soldier would want to hear from his girl.

In Vietnam itself, perhaps the most popular song among the troops had an unmistakable message. Sung by the Animals, the refrain was powerful:

> We gotta get out of this place
> If it's the last thing we ever do

We gotta get out of this place
Girl, there's a better life for me and you

There was another resonant song in-country: "Green, Green Grass of Home," a haunting, fatalistic ballad told, it's revealed in the final verse, by a death-row inmate facing execution. Porter Wagoner sang one version, Tom Jones another. For soldiers who themselves felt under a kind of death sentence, the song spoke volumes.

"Music doesn't create movements," the scholar and historian Craig Werner says, "but if a movement exists, it can power and drive that movement." In the case of the Vietnam War, music powered and drove not only antiwar sentiment but also the cause of civil rights and issues of race. In 1968, James Brown released "Say It Loud—I'm Black and I'm Proud," which resonated at home and in Southeast Asia, and his "Papa's Got a Brand New Bag" was part of the soundtrack of the Black Power Movement.

GREEN, GREEN GRASS OF HOME and GALVESTON

I love classic country music, and it gets no better than "Green, Green Grass of Home." Curly Putman's lyrics paint a detailed picture of life, before revealing it's just a dream. At the end the narrator looks back and wonders if he focused on what really mattered. It speaks to many of us, I think, because we all have some of that kind of regret. Like "We Gotta Get Out of This Place," "Green, Green Grass" was adopted by soldiers because the lyrics resonated with their plight in the field—examples of how great songs can be applied to different situations and contexts.

Written by Jimmy Webb and popularized by Glen Campbell, whom I revere, "Galveston" was, like "Fortunate Son," explicitly about the war ("I clean my gun and dream of Galveston").

Later, Campbell would do a different, but more emotional, live version, accompanied by an orchestra, and with a dramatically slowed-down tempo. I find this version haunting, and it allows you to pull out the meaning of each word with Campbell's flawless and raw emotional vocal.   —T.M.

As his Rock & Roll Hall of Fame biography tells us, "What became known as soul music in the sixties, funk music in the seventies, and rap music in the eighties is directly attributable to James Brown"—the Godfather of Soul. "His transformation of gospel fervor into the taut, explosive intensity of rhythm & blues, combined with precision choreography and dynamic showmanship, served to define the directions black music would take from the release of his first R&B hit ('Please Please Please') in 1956 to the present day." Politically, he'd made his mark early. "By the late Sixties," the Rock & Roll Hall of Fame says, "Brown had attained the status of a musical and cultural revolutionary, owing to his message of black pride and self-sufficiency."

WE GOTTA GET OUT OF THIS PLACE

This song, which became an anthem for Vietnam soldiers and antiwar protesters, was written by one of the most successful songwriting teams of all time, husband and wife Barry Mann and Cynthia Weil.

"We Gotta Get Out of This Place" was an anthem for Vietnam soldiers and antiwar protesters. As the story goes, the writers intended to pitch it to the Righteous Brothers, and then Mann considered recording it himself. But before he could, the Animals' producer, Mickie Most, recorded it. The lyrics were tweaked and the sound incorporated the working-class roots of the band members.

Bruce Springsteen credits this song as one of his biggest influences. The bass line hits you immediately. Sparse, the track begins to build over the gritty vocal of Eric Burdon. The tension increases until the chorus takes hold and the music moves into the background and closes with the line: "Girl, there's a better life for me and you," wrapping up the sentiment of the song perfectly.   —T.M.

The Animals sang "We Gotta Get Out of This Place," which Vietnam veterans recalled as the defining song of the war.

In an interview with Craig Werner and Doug Bradley for their study *We Gotta Get Out of This Place,* John Martinez, a musician who served as a machine gunner in Vietnam, recalled the cacophony of Qui Nhon. "[A] lot of times at night,"

Martinez said, "the white guys would hang out in one area, the blacks in another. The southerners listening to country and playing poker. The black guys were listening to Aretha and James Brown."

James Brown (shown performing in Vietnam in 1968) and Aretha Franklin were central figures in the changing America of the sixties and beyond.

Aretha: That's all he had to call her. Everybody knew—and knows—who he meant. In her "Chain of Fools," she sang a kind of R&B version of Seeger's "Waist Deep in the Big Muddy," a song that its audience in Vietnam interpreted as an indictment of failed leadership. There was, though, a note of hope in "Chain of Fools": Franklin predicted that one day the chain would break and the captives would go free—or, in terms of the war, go home. "I've had a lot of servicemen—Vietnam vets—come up to me and tell me how much my music meant to them over there," Franklin recalled. "I'm sure all those guys were in a lot of pain, something you or I can't imagine." To assuage—or to try to assuage—that pain, GIs listened to Otis Redding, who'd written "Respect," and his and Steve Cropper's "(Sittin' on) The Dock of the Bay," and to Simon and Garfunkel's "Bridge Over Troubled Water" and "Homeward Bound," which was all they wanted to be.

A young female protester takes her stand in front of armed police at an antiwar rally at the 1968 Democratic National Convention in Chicago.

SINGIN' IN VIETNAM TALKIN' BLUES

Johnny Cash. The Man in Black. Truly an iconic artist and totally underrated as a songwriter.

"Singin' in Vietnam Talkin' Blues" is intriguing because it's the only recitation song we have highlighted. It was inspired by a trip Cash and his wife, June Carter Cash, took to Vietnam to entertain the troops. The choice of a recitation (and incorporating that very idea into the title) tells me he wanted the lyrics to dramatically rise above the musical side of the record. It's as if he's having a conversation with us about what he saw and felt. This isn't a studio track; it's from the heart. He tells us in the song they were scared when they heard bombs exploding at night, which isn't exactly what you'd expect from Johnny Cash. And yet with that booming voice, it's impossible not to feel the pain he felt for the troops, and the fear that anybody under fire would experience.
—T.M.

Johnny Cash was a unique figure, but his views on the war were fairly representative. Neither a ferocious hawk nor a reflexive dove, Cash toured the Far East for the USO and left us an intriguing canon about the era. "Cash was greatly troubled by the Vietnam War," the biographer Robert Hilburn wrote in *Johnny Cash: The Life.* "His natural instinct was to support his country at all costs, but his visits to hospitals and talks with soldiers hit him hard, and he admitted his doubts to his brother Tommy. 'Maybe,' he said, 'they may be dying for a cause that isn't just.'" In "What Is Truth?" he meditated on the generation gap, and his "Singin' in Vietnam Talkin' Blues" gave Cash the chance to talk about his time in the war zone—his "little trip into a living hell."

In 1974, the year Nixon was forced from office, Cash wrote a more traditionally patriotic song, "Ragged Old Flag":

> You see, we got a little hole in that flag there
> When Washington took it across the Delaware.
> And it got powder-burned the night Francis Scott Key
> Sat watching it writing *Say Can You See.*
> And it got a bad rip in New Orleans
> With Pakenham and Jackson tuggin' at its seams.
> And it almost fell at the Alamo
> Beside the Texas flag, but she waved on though
> She got cut with a sword at Chancellorsville
> And she got cut again at Shiloh Hill.
> There was Robert E. Lee, Beauregard, and Bragg
> And the south wind blew hard on that *Ragged Old Flag.*
> On Flanders field in World War One
> She got a big hole from a Bertha Gun.
> She turned blood red in World War Two,
> She hung limp, and low, by the time it was through.
> She was in Korea and Vietnam,
> She went where she was sent by Uncle Sam.
> Native Americans, brown, yellow and white
> All shed blood for the Stars and Stripes.
> In her own good land here she's been abused,
> She's been burned, dishonored, denied, and refused.
> And the government for which she stands
> Has been scandalized throughout the land.
> And she's getting threadbare, and wearing thin,

But she's in good shape, for the shape she's in.
'Cause she's been through the fire before,
And I believe she can take a whole lot more.

"Ragged Old Flag" is a complex piece—a defense of the flag at a time when it's "been abused / She's been burned, dishonored, denied, and refused," while also calling Nixon's lies to account: "And the government for which she stands / Has been scandalized throughout the land." That Cash sang of the flag's being "ragged" is key to the song's power—in Cash's take, the Stars and Stripes wasn't a window decal but an emblem of an ethos of liberty that had to be fought for. Taken all in all, the song captures Cash's ambivalence about American glory and American sin: "But she's in good shape, for the shape she's in."

Johnny Cash's *Ragged Old Flag* album cover.

Late in his life, in 1993, Cash recorded an elegiac song about Vietnam, "Drive On," which was laced with the same sense of tragedy. Life will never be what we want it to be, and the best we can do, in the end, is to endure, seeking love in a fallen world that's destined to disappoint us.

Considering the source, it was a startling claim. A longtime lieutenant of Time-Life founder Henry Luce, journalist Richard Clurman found himself chatting one day in the late 1960s with Leonard Bernstein, the legendary composer and conductor of the New York Philharmonic.

"Elvis Presley," Bernstein said, "is the greatest cultural force in the twentieth century."

Taken aback, Clurman, who recounted the exchange to the writer David Halberstam, offered an alternative.

"What about Picasso?"

"No, it's Elvis," Bernstein replied. "He introduced the beat to everything and he changed everything—music, language, clothes, it's a whole new social revolution—the Sixties comes from it."

The Presley legend has proven durable and intriguing not least because it mirrors much of American culture in his lifetime and beyond. His fantastic rise and his long sad slide, in his later years, into an overweight, gun-toting, prescription-drug-abusing conspiracy theorist about communism and the counterculture (he hated the Beatles, once telling President Nixon that the British band threatened American values) tap into fundamental questions about race, mass culture, sexuality, and working-class anxiety in postwar America. A poor boy made good in the prosperous fifties, Presley experienced tension and feared disorder in the sixties before breaking down totally in the hectic seventies. In his music and in his movies, in his private worlds at Graceland and in Las Vegas,

Presley was a forerunner of the reality-TV era, in which celebrities play an outsize role in the imaginative lives of their fans.

He was born in 1935 in Tupelo, Mississippi, in the hilly upcountry region of the state the writer Julia Reed has described as the "Balkans of the South." (The other two distinct Mississippi worlds are the Delta and the Gulf Coast.) His father struggled to eke out a living, working different jobs and signing up for FDR's Works Progress Administration after doing time at Mississippi's Parchman Farm prison for forging a check. His mother was devoted to her son, all the more so because Presley had a twin brother who was stillborn. Elvis grew up as a member of the Assembly of God, a denomination that emphasized personal religious experiences. Music and singing were essential means of creating ecstatic moments of transcendence; it was a vibrant, emotional, very public form of faith. The individual was the vessel of the Holy Spirit—a performer, if only for the congregation, and Presley absorbed both white and Black gospel in Mississippi.

Eventually the family moved to Memphis, which was perfect for Presley. A longtime cotton hub, the city, like Presley himself, sat between the blues-soaked Delta and the virtually all-white country world of Nashville. In the summer of 1954, after a brief, not-

"Elvis Presley," Leonard Bernstein said, "is the greatest cultural force in the twentieth century."

quite-successful visit the year before, Presley cut a record with the producer Sam Phillips, who ran Sun Records on Union Avenue.

A few days later, at an open-air performance at the Overton Shell in Memphis, Presley played the two songs from that recording. As Joel Williamson, the scholar of Southern history, observed, Presley took "That's All Right" (written by an African American blues musician, Arthur Crudup) and the flip side, "Blue Moon of Kentucky" (written by a white bluegrass man, Bill Monroe), and made them his own. "Elvis, using his God-given rich and versatile voice, perfected by practice, gave [the songs] a different turn," Williamson wrote. "Just as 'That's All Right' was not black anymore, 'Blue Moon' was no longer hillbilly; it was joyous, country-come-to-town and damn glad to be there." The audience, led by the ecstatic young women in the crowd, went wild. "I was scared stiff," Presley recalled. "Everyone was hollering, and I didn't know what they were hollering at."

They were, of course, hollering at *him,* transported by his electric physicality and his extraordinary voice, which ranged comfortably from baritone to tenor and above. He did not simply sing. He became the music, as though possessed by a spirit of joy and release back at the Assembly of God. It was sexual, yes, and thus disturbing to the more placid and puritanical of observers, but it was inescapably religious, too, in the sense that religion evokes realities ordinarily hidden from the human eye. Here, on a stage in a park near the banks of the Mississippi in western Tennessee, was something new in American popular culture: a white man drawing on the deep tradition of African American blues and making it his own. In the popular mind, a fresh genre—a different epoch—was coming into being. "Hearing him for the first time," Bob Dylan said, "was like busting out of jail."

A white man singing traditionally Black music; a young performer producing sexual heat; a Southern kid going national: little wonder Presley struck so many as so refreshing in the mid-1950s. On September 9, 1956, Presley made his first appearance on *The Ed Sullivan Show,* producing an 82.6 percent television rating.

His second turn on the show was also a blockbuster, and by the time Presley sang for Sullivan on a third occasion—the one where CBS directed that the cameras show Presley only from the waist up—the buttoned-down host had been won over. "I wanted to say to Elvis Presley and the country," Sullivan intoned, "that this is a real decent, fine boy."

His evident religious commitment also helped Presley win broader acceptance. As with so many Southern men, he could seem equally at home in church on Sunday mornings as in the juke joints on Saturday nights (even if he didn't actually turn up in church much as he grew older). Americans are familiar with the type. We had one for president for two terms at the close of the twentieth century: Bill Clinton, whose mother, Virginia, positively worshipped Elvis. "I loved Elvis," Bill Clinton recalled in his presidential memoir. "I could sing all his songs. . . . Beyond his music, I identified with his small-town southern roots." And like Clinton, Presley was a model compartmentalizer. In Presley's case, he created music that celebrated a freer, more open attitude toward sex, while simultaneously releasing popular gospel tracks. As has often been remarked of charismatic figures such as the fictional James Bond and the real-life Presley, women wanted to be with him; men just wanted to be him.

Presley had been born into the demographic that helped elect Nixon—the ones who didn't protest, who didn't grow their hair long, who didn't burn their draft cards or run the country down (basically the Okies from Muskogee).

Like the nation itself in the years of Vietnam and of Watergate, Presley was torn between patriotism and self-indulgence, clinging sentimentally to an older, warmer vision of America as he fed his own appetites for opioids and for fried peanut butter and banana sandwiches. Presley's own contradictions were like the country's as it hurtled—even stumbled—through a difficult and self-involved era.

* * *

If Presley and Nixon represented one pole of American life, their antithesis could be found at the Woodstock Music and Art Fair in upstate New York in 1969.

The three-day festival featured Richie Havens, Sweetwater, Bert Sommer, Ravi Shankar, Tim Hardin, Melanie Safka, Arlo Guthrie, Joan Baez (who sang "Swing Low, Sweet Chariot" and "We Shall Overcome"), Quill, Country Joe Mc-Donald, Santana, John Sebastian, the Keef Hartley Band, the Incredible String Band, Canned Heat, Mountain, the Grateful Dead, Creedence Clearwater Revival, the Who, Jefferson Airplane, Joe Cocker, Country Joe and the Fish, Janis Joplin, Ten Years After, the Band, Johnny Winter, Sly & the Family Stone, Blood, Sweat & Tears, Crosby, Stills, Nash & Young, Paul Butterfield Blues Band, and Sha Na Na. Joni Mitchell wasn't there—she had stayed in New York City in order to be certain of making a scheduled appearance on *The Dick Cavett Show*—but afterward wrote a song, "Woodstock," that portrayed the festival in terms of a generation's mythic (but doomed) effort to return to a garden of innocence. "Her version of the song is a modal dirge," David Yaffe wrote in his *Reckless Daughter: A Portrait of Joni Mitchell.* "It can be played on nothing but the black keys on the piano—a minor chord, a suspended chord, and moving down to the ninth chord. . . . It is a purgation. It is an omen that something very, very bad will happen when the mud dries and the hippies go home. That garden they had to get back to—it was an illusion."

In the last performance of the event, Jimi Hendrix made a bit of history with an electric instrumental rendition of "The Star-Spangled Banner" on his guitar. "You can leave if you want to," Hendrix had told the crowd. "We're just jamming, that's all. Okay? You can leave, or you can clap." He was playing in the early-morning hours of the last day of the festival—it had run over schedule so badly that Hendrix, who'd been slated to appear at 11:00 P.M. the evening before, did not go onstage until 8:00 A.M. Hendrix's "Star-Spangled Banner" was a show-stopper. "The song had long been a showcase for Jimi to display his innovative

CHAPTER EIGHT

BORN IN THE U.S.A.

She's still a beacon, still a magnet for all who must have freedom, for all the
pilgrims from all the lost places who are hurtling through the darkness, toward
home.

    —RONALD REAGAN, Farewell Address to the Nation, 1989

Of the many tragic images of that day, the picture I couldn't let go of was of
the emergency workers going *up* the stairs as others rushed down to safety. . . .
If you love life or any part of it, the depth of their sacrifice is unthinkable and
incomprehensible.

    —BRUCE SPRINGSTEEN on the terrorist attacks of September 11, 2001

In the summer of 1984, the conservative columnist George F. Will attended—
and, even more remarkably, enjoyed—a Bruce Springsteen concert in suburban
Washington. It was a late-August "Born in the U.S.A." show.

 In his concertgoing costume of a bow tie and double-breasted blazer, Will was
playing to type and acknowledged that Springsteen's fans "regarded me as exotic
fauna . . . and undertook to instruct me." He reported a "typical tutorial":

  "What do you like about him?"
  Male fan: "He sings about faith and traditional values."

Nearly 3,000 people died in the attacks of Tuesday, September 11, 2001—
what President Bush would call a "day of fire."

Male fan's female friend, dryly: "And cars and girls."

Male fan: "No, no, it's about community and roots and perseverance and family."

She: "And cars and girls."

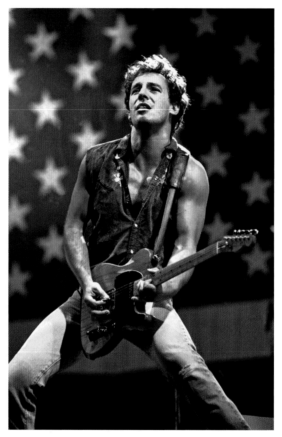

Bruce Springsteen in a performance of "Born in the U.S.A.," Los Angeles, 1985.

Will took Springsteen's work ethic as a manifestation of the virtues of the free market. "In an age of lackadaisical effort and slipshod products, anyone who does anything—anything legal—conspicuously well and with zest is a national asset,"

Will wrote. "Springsteen's tour is hard, honest work and evidence of the astonishing vitality of America's regions and generations. They produce distinctive tones of voice that other regions and generations embrace. There still is nothing quite like being born in the U.S.A."

True, but Will's conservative take on Springsteen's oeuvre elided the complexities of the lyrics themselves. A son of blue-collar New Jersey, Springsteen had long sung of working-class anxiety.

To Springsteen, "Born in the U.S.A." was, he recalled in his memoir, "a protest song, and when I heard it thundering back at me through the Hit Factory's gargantuan studio speakers, I knew it was one of the best things I'd ever done. It was a GI blues, the verses an accounting, the choruses a declaration of the one sure thing that could not be denied . . . birthplace. Birthplace, and the right to all of the blood, confusion, blessings and grace that come with it. Having paid body and soul, you have earned, many times over, the right to claim and shape your piece of home ground."

In the aftermath of George Will's encounter with the "Born in the U.S.A." tour, the reelection campaign of Reagan and George H. W. Bush, which was then under way against the Democratic ticket of Walter Mondale and Geraldine Ferraro, sought to adopt Springsteen, and his song, as its own. In a speech at Hammonton, New Jersey, on Wednesday, September 19, 1984, Reagan said, "America's future rests in a thousand dreams inside your hearts; it rests in the message of hope in songs so many young Americans admire: New Jersey's own Bruce Springsteen. And helping you make those dreams come true is what this job of mine is all about."

Springsteen was having none of it.

In a *Rolling Stone* interview, Springsteen said, "I think what's happening now is people want to forget," he told the magazine. "There was Vietnam, there was Watergate, there was Iran—we were beaten, we were hustled, and then we were humiliated. And I think people have a need to feel good about the country they live in. But what's happening, I think, is that the need—which is a good thing—is gettin' manipulated and exploited. And you see the Reagan reelection ads on TV—you know, 'It's morning in America.' And you say, well, it's not morning in Pittsburgh. It's not morning above 125th Street in New York. It's midnight, and, like, there's a bad moon risin'. And that's why when Reagan mentioned my name in New Jersey, I felt it was another manipulation, and I had to disassociate myself from the president's kind words."

The country Reagan was to lead was suffering from what his predecessor, Jimmy Carter, had described, in July 1979, as a "crisis of confidence." As the 1970s ended, inflation spiked, interest rates soared, the Soviets invaded Afghanistan, and Islamic militants took U.S. diplomats hostage in Iran. Carter would be the fifth American president in twenty years. "The erosion of our confidence in the future," he told the country in mid-1979, "is threatening to destroy the social and the political fabric of America."

A former movie actor, television host (*General Electric Theater* and *Death Valley Days*), corporate spokesman, and governor of California, Reagan was in many ways a conservative reply to Roosevelt's New Deal, Harry Truman's Fair Deal, and Lyndon Johnson's Great Society. "No government ever voluntarily reduces itself in size," Reagan said in a televised speech on behalf of Barry Goldwater's presidential campaign in late October 1964. "Government programs, once launched, never disappear. Actually, a government bureau is the nearest thing to eternal life we'll ever see on this earth."

His critique was couched in the language of American optimism. "You and I are told increasingly that we have to choose between a left or right, but I would like to suggest that there is no such thing as a left or right," Reagan said. "There is only an up or down—up to a man's age-old dream, the ultimate in individual freedom consistent with law and order—or down to the ant heap of totalitarianism, and regardless of their sincerity, their humanitarian motives, those who would trade our freedom for security have embarked on this downward course."

Reagan, then, should have been a divisive politician—a man about whom the nation was closely and bitterly split. In the White House, he'd prove a contradictory figure. He mangled facts; caricatured welfare recipients; presided over a dark recession in 1981–82; seemed uncaring about the emerging HIV/AIDS crisis; and plunged the country into the Iran-Contra scandal. And yet while many people were consistently critical of him, he left office with a 63 percent approval rating. The man himself seemed to dwell just above the arena, escaping widespread political enmity.

The song most associated with the Reagan vision can be seen as a conservative "Born in the U.S.A."—Lee Greenwood's "God Bless the U.S.A." Greenwood had toiled for nearly two decades as a Las Vegas lounge singer (and occasional card dealer) before finding success in Nashville and winning the 1983 Country Music Association Male Vocalist of the Year award.

"The song was a response to the hurt and anger I felt after the [Soviet] downing of a Korean jet on a flight from New York to Seoul in 1983, with 269 passengers aboard, including 63 Americans," Greenwood recalled. "I could not forget the scenes of weeping men, women, and children who had just been told the grim news that their loved ones would never return." Looking back on "God Bless the U.S.A.," Greenwood mused, "Did I know the song was special, a hit from the beginning? Well, every time you go into the studio to record a song, you think it is going to be a hit. But, yes, I knew this song was special because of the response we received whenever we sang it live."

As the 1984 presidential race took shape, Reagan ad maestro Sig Rogich happened to hear Greenwood's "God Bless the U.S.A." Rogich knew it would be a fantastic score for the Reagan "It's Morning in America" campaign, and he called Greenwood the next day to see if he could use the song in commercials for the president. Thrilled, the singer licensed it to the campaign for a dollar.

BORN IN THE U.S.A. and GOD BLESS THE U.S.A.

The parallels here pretty much stop with the titles. Greenwood's "God Bless the U.S.A." is an extremely patriotic, borderline over-the-top anthem that still ensures a standing ovation when performed today. It was a huge hit and has become a Red State favorite. Springsteen's "Born in the U.S.A." was a working-class song, a blue-collar anthem detailing the mistreatment of returning Vietnam War veterans.   —T.M.

It quickly became the Reagan-Bush reelection anthem and is now a conservative standard. Greenwood's song was as unapologetically upbeat about America in the Age of Reagan as George Cohan had been in World War I and Irving Berlin had been in World War II and Barry Sadler had been in the Vietnam era. Though there's no ambivalence in "God Bless the U.S.A." about the national enterprise, the song's optimism isn't entirely schmaltzy. In the opening lyrics, the narrator muses about what he'd do if he lost everything and had to begin again. The song's solution to the hypothetical problem is one that could resonate with liberals as well as conservatives, Democrats as well as Republicans, for the answer to the doomsday scenario is one with deep roots in the American experience: He'd take advantage of the America of second chances and hurl himself back into the arena.

The imagined nation of "God Bless the U.S.A." is one of opportunity, a place where Americans, to borrow a phrase of Lincoln's, have a "fair chance" to rise and thrive. There's no impenetrable darkness in Greenwood's song, only crises to be overcome in a land secured by sacrifice and open to all. Where Springsteen sang of broken promises and unfulfilled dreams, Greenwood insisted on perpetual promise and enduring dreams. Neither was wholly right or wholly wrong; the country works for some and doesn't work for others, which is in the nature of things. Like America, the songs are a matter of emphasis and of perspective.

"And so, goodbye": President Reagan prepares to deliver his farewell address, Wednesday, January 11, 1989.

reenwood's perspective on the country was Reagan's. There were, as always, other perspectives—many others—and one of the most influential was that of Run-DMC, a pioneering rap group that played a critical role in the rise of hip-hop. In 1983, Run-DMC indicted "the way it is" in "It's Like That." (Grandmaster Flash and the Furious Five's "The Message" was a similar number.)

Lee Greenwood performs his signature "God Bless the U.S.A." at a Reagan centennial celebration at the fortieth president's Simi Valley, California, library in 2011.

Hip-hop's initial commercial and cultural success was roughly concurrent with the Reagan presidency. "The sharp contrast between a White House that is announcing 'Morning in America' and a Black culture that is mourning the racial divides in this country was clear from the beginning," the professor and scholar Michael Eric Dyson says. "You get the politicization from the start. When Chuck D said rap music is the CNN of Black America, he understood that hip-hop is both the reality of the streets and, for white America, a window on that reality. It is a sonic fiction being generated to tell the truth about Black folk in America, and therefore about America itself."

There were, to be sure, sundry truths. Artists such as Jay-Z, Snoop Dogg, Lauryn Hill, and Queen Latifah built cultural bridges once thought fanciful. "They taught Black America an important lesson: You don't have to cross over to white America; you can get white America to cross over to you," Dyson says. "Rappers were talking about these enclaves of civic horror called ghettoes and slums and, by owning the story, were restoring the humanity and agency of a Black culture." And there were gangsta songs like N.W.A's "Fuck tha Police" on their album *Straight Outta Compton* and Ice-T's "Squeeze the Trigger."

Tupac Shakur's incandescent poetry exemplified the fury and the fire of the emerging world of hip-hop in the post-Reagan years.

The power of hip-hop has shaped each post-Reagan generation. Urgent and energetic, rap music is protest itself. Tupac Shakur's 1991 "Words of Wisdom," for instance, is fiery poetry. "What's more a part of the American Dream than these guys from nothing, seeking everything and not letting anything get in their way?" Dyson says. " 'My community, my street, my hood'—there's a path from Run-DMC to Obama running for president. What hip-hop did was create an image in the minds of young white people that a smart Black guy could talk intelligently. There would have been no Obama without Jay Z."

Tuesday, September 11, 2001, dawned bright and blue, and it promised to be a beautiful late-summer day. American Airlines Flight 11, nonstop from Boston to LAX, took off at 7:59 A.M. Eastern time. A passenger named Mohammed Atta was in business class, in seat 8D. Within fifteen minutes, the jet had reached 26,000 feet. About sixteen seconds later, air traffic control in Boston issued a routine directive to the pilots to head up to 35,000 feet.

No one replied. Flight 11 had gone dark.

Reports of what happened between 8:14 and 8:46, reconstructed by the 9/11 Commission, come from flight attendants who called the ground as the hijacking unfolded. There were stabbings and the spraying of Mace; the taking of the cockpit; and Atta's assumption of the controls. As the plane headed toward New York, officials on the ground thought the hijackers might be bound for Kennedy Airport. The rest of the story is in the words of Madeline "Amy" Sweeney, one of the flight attendants still on a phone line. "Something is wrong. We are in a rapid descent . . . we are all over the place." It was about 8:44. "We are flying low. We are flying very, very low. We are flying way too low." A pause, then: "Oh my God, we are way too low." American Flight 11 struck the North Tower of the World Trade Center at 8:46:40, and the world changed.

The faraway fanatic—the elusive embodiment of ancient evil in a new century, the man and his followers who made a living hell of Sweeney's final moments—met his own end on Monday, May 2, 2011, when American military forces, in a nighttime raid, killed him in a walled compound along a dirt road in Pakistan. Osama bin Laden, the terrorist leader in his early fifties who seemed somehow ageless, was shot in the chest and head and buried at sea. Amy Sweeney and the roughly three thousand other victims of 9/11—as well as the victims of bin Laden's other attacks, from East Africa to Yemen—were avenged.

The second tower of the World Trade Center explodes. "Where were you," Alan Jackson would ask in song, "when the world stopped turnin'?"

Bin Laden had declared war on the West, especially on America. He claimed he was doing so in the name of Allah. The extreme reading of Islam that provided him his rhetoric and his ethos, however, was secondary to the more elemental force that drove him: the will to power. The failure to capture or kill him sooner flummoxed three presidential administrations, from Bill Clinton to

Barack Obama. In retrospect (that wondrous thing), we can see how bin Laden moved from smaller-scale bombings, especially the 1998 attacks on American embassies in Africa, to what Al Qaeda called the "spectacular" misery of 9/11.

Americans like to look to tomorrow. It's the frontier spirit in us, the restlessness that brought so many to the New World from the Old. But without remembering yesterday, we may fail to learn from even the very recent past. For Americans in the nineteenth century, slavery and the Civil War were shaping events; in the middle of the twentieth century, there were Munich and Pearl Harbor and then Vietnam; now there is 9/11 and its fallout, not least the Iraq War.

Our central yesterday remains that now-distant Tuesday in 2001. It is the day that has affected every subsequent day, from Manhattan to Kabul to Baghdad to Islamabad. At the heart of the story of that day are people like Peter Hanson, a passenger on United Airlines Flight 175, the plane that hit the South Tower nearly twenty minutes after Amy Sweeney's American Airlines jet struck the North Tower. In a call to his father, Lee, seconds before the end, Peter said: "It's getting bad, Dad—a stewardess was stabbed . . . It's getting very bad on the plane . . . I think we are going down . . . Don't worry, Dad—if it happens, it'll be very fast—my God my God."

It did happen. On the Friday after the attacks, George W. Bush stepped up to the lectern of Washington National Cathedral to address a nation in shock. The memorial service for the victims of Tuesday's horrors alternated between mourning and resolve. The congregation sang "O God, Our Help in Ages Past" and "A Mighty Fortress Is Our God"; it listened to solo renditions of Katharine Lee Bates's "America the Beautiful," Albert Malotte's setting of "The Lord's Prayer," and a U.S. Army Orchestra performance of Berlin's "God Bless America."

As the service came to a close, the congregation sang the hymn that had been composed by Julia Ward Howe in a distant Washington night at Willard's Hotel: "Mine eyes have seen the glory of the coming of the Lord. . . ."

"I can hear you," President Bush cried through the bullhorn at Ground Zero. "The rest of the world hears you, and the people who knocked these buildings down will hear all of us soon."

There had been some behind-the-scenes debate about the hymn's verses. Some White House staffers and cathedral officials had quietly objected to the martial nature of Ward's poem. Its "words and images were unabashedly militant," as John Stauffer and Benjamin Soskis wrote in a study of "The Battle Hymn," and Karen Hughes, a senior adviser to President Bush, "felt the need to run the selection by the president. She let him know that some churches considered the song excessively bellicose and had removed it from their hymnals." Bush was unfazed. "Defiance," he told Hughes, "is good." The hymn would be sung—including the unflinching "As He died to make men holy / Let us die to make men free."

From "The Lord's Prayer" to "The Battle Hymn of the Republic," the music of the day reflected the hour's complex emotions.

Beyond the cathedral, many Americans turned to music to make sense of the deadliest single-day attack on America since Pearl Harbor. On Friday, September 21, 2001, in a broadcast entitled "America: A Tribute to Heroes," musicians sought to console and to inspire. Performers included Springsteen ("My City of Ruins"), Stevie Wonder and Take 6 ("Love's in Need of Love Today"), U2 ("Peace on Earth"; "Walk On"), Faith Hill ("There Will Come a Day"), Tom Petty and the Heartbreakers ("I Won't Back Down"), Enrique Iglesias ("Hero"), Neil Young ("Imagine"), Alicia Keys ("Someday We'll All Be Free"), Limp Bizkit and John Rzeznik ("Wish You Were Here"), Billy Joel ("New York State of Mind"), the Dixie Chicks ("I Believe in Love"), Dave Matthews ("Everyday"), Wyclef Jean ("Redemption Song"), Mariah Carey ("Hero"), Bon Jovi ("Livin' on a Prayer"), Sheryl Crow ("Safe and Sound"), Sting ("Fragile"), Eddie Vedder ("Long Road"), Paul Simon ("Bridge Over Troubled Water"), Celine Dion ("God Bless America"), and Willie Nelson with the company ("America the Beautiful").

The details of what President Bush would call a "day of fire" found expression in new music. When reports came of Todd Beamer's final words—"Let's roll"—as he and passengers aboard United Airlines Flight 93 stormed the cockpit in the skies above Pennsylvania, Neil Young, who had been similarly moved by the Kent State shootings thirty years before, wrote "Let's Roll," an anthem about the courage of Beamer and his compatriots.

Young was telling the story of Flight 93's martyred heroes; in "Where Were You (When the World Stopped Turning)?" Alan Jackson sang about the impact of the day on the rest of us. By asking the question of his audience—Where were you?—Jackson brought the whole country into the story of the day and affirmed the centrality of things we tend to take for granted. Part of Jackson's chorus was from St. Paul's First Letter to the Corinthians: "And now these three remain: faith, hope, and love. But the greatest of these is love."

Where Jackson was warm, his fellow country artist Toby Keith was warlike. In "Courtesy of the Red, White and Blue (The Angry American)" Keith was martial, plain-spoken, and provocative. His was an anthem not of anguish but of anger. The essayist Verlyn Klinkenborg wrote of catching Keith's singing the song on Country Music Television in the summer of 2002. "Mr. Keith is a solid slab of a man, a former football player and Oklahoma oilhand," Klinkenborg wrote. "On CMT he wore a flat-crowned, pure-white cowboy hat and a long goatee that was half Buffalo Bill, half buffalo. He struck out into the song, and the audience sang along with him. The music was solemn, almost dirge-like. Imagine, if you can, a cross between the slow part of 'American Pie' and 'Ballad of the Green Berets.' "

These were voices from Nashville; in New Jersey, Bruce Springsteen meditated on the firefighters and the cops who had laid down their lives for others. "Of the many tragic images of that day, the picture I couldn't let go of was of the emergency workers going *up* the stairs as others rushed down to safety," Springsteen recalled. His "Into the Fire," on the 2002 album *The Rising,* was an ode to those heroes. In addition to the title track, *The Rising* also featured "My City of Ruins" and "Lonesome Day," songs that were heard in the context of the opening years of the war on terror, a struggle that brought its own ambiguities and uncertainties. Neither as unified as in World War II nor as overwhelmingly divided as in Vietnam, the post-9/11 nation was the kind of place Springsteen had sung about so long: searching and wondering, nostalgic and nervous.

THE RISING

In the Grammy Award–winning album *The Rising,* released about ten months after 9/11, Springsteen's great songwriting tells you how you feel about something in a way you didn't even know how to express.

He gives us a modern-day hymnal with this body of work, with words and music to grieve 9/11, along with a sense of community that we're going to get through it, together. The chorus of "Into the Fire," an ode to the more than 300 firefighters lost that awful day, transforms the pain of losing these brave heroes into a mantra of hope.

"My City of Ruins" is another favorite from this album. Written before 9/11, it takes on a broader impact from its original purpose (to draw attention to the revitalization of Asbury Park). The city is the people, with words to come back stronger than ever. It's understandable how these songs have come to be anthems for the brave men and women of the New York fire and police departments. Rise up. —T.M.

There were flashes of controversy that were reminiscent of the 1960s and early '70s. In 2003, as U.S. troops prepared to invade Saddam Hussein's Iraq, the Dixie Chicks protested President Bush's leadership. "Just so you know, we're on the good side with y'all," Natalie Maines said from the stage during a performance in London. "We do not want this war, this violence, and we're ashamed that the president of the United States is from Texas." Facing a fan backlash and boycotts—including being pulled from many radio playlists—Maines said, "We are currently in Europe and witnessing a huge anti-American sentiment as a result of the perceived rush to war. While war may remain a viable option, as a mother, I just want to see every possible alternative exhausted before children and American soldiers' lives are lost. I love my country. I am a proud American."

It wasn't enough. "As a concerned American citizen, I apologize to President Bush because my remark was disrespectful," Maines said in a subsequent statement. Three years later, she would un-apologize, saying, "I don't feel he is owed any respect whatsoever."

The iconic *Entertainment Weekly* cover shot, photographed by James White, after Natalie Maines of the Dixie Chicks said they were "ashamed" of George W. Bush and the march to war in Iraq in 2003.

"I mean, the Dixie Chicks are free to speak their mind," Bush replied when asked about Maines's London comment. "They can say what they want to say. . . . That's the great thing about America. It stands in stark contrast to Iraq, by the way."

Toby Keith was a bit less nuanced in his reaction. In 2002, Maines had dismissed Keith's "Courtesy of the Red, White and Blue" as "ignorant," adding, "It targets an entire culture—and not just the bad people who did bad things." Now, after London, Keith fired back by flashing a manufactured image of Maines with Saddam Hussein on huge screens as he sang "Courtesy" in concert.

The episode—the Dixie Chicks call it "the Incident" (with a capital "I")—raised profound questions about free speech and its implications. There were death threats and slurs, angry call-ins and widespread censorship. Attacked as "hillbilly Jane Fondas," the Chicks were photographed nude for the May 2, 2003, cover of *Entertainment Weekly* with terms like "Saddam's Angels," "Traitors," "Hero," "Dixie Sluts," and "Proud Americans" written on their bodies.

The controversy was a perfect storm. The antiwar, anti-Bush sentiments were expressed not in song, where they might have been less incendiary, but as a remark from the stage in a foreign country, which was off-putting to people inclined to be outraged in the first place. And they came as the cultural divides between what we now call Red and Blue America were growing, with country fans predominately tending to be red state folks. (The dichotomy comes from the color the networks use on their election-night maps to show which candidate has won which state.)

In a column published on the Country Music Television website, the writer Chet Flippo gave Maines a tutorial on the dynamics of protest. "What do you expect country fans to say when a country star dumps on the president?" Flippo wrote. "That audience is tolerant of artists' mistakes and foibles: drunkenness, drug use, adultery, no-shows and any amount of indulgent behavior. What that audience will not tolerate is an artist turning on that audience. And Maines's attack on Bush was in effect a direct attack on the country audience. And its values. And its patriotism . . . Memo to Natalie Maines: You're an artist? And you have a message? Hey, put it in a song. We'll listen to that. But, otherwise—shut up and sing."

The Chicks had red-state roots but now needed blue-state support to stay alive professionally. In 2006 they released an album and a defiant single, "Not Ready to Make Nice," and did well at the Grammys the following year. Country music, however, never welcomed them back, and the break between one of the most commercially successful female groups in history and the prevailing culture of red-state America is a case study in a polarization that endures nearly two decades on.

The two men could hardly have been more different. One the fatherless son of a single mother, the other a scion of the most important American political family since the Adamses; one a cool, intellectual analyst, the other an instinctive gut player who didn't look back once a decision was made. Yet there they were, together in the East Room of the White House on a May day in 2012, inexorably linked by history: Barack Hussein Obama and George Walker Bush.

The occasion was the unveiling of George Bush's and Laura Bush's White House portraits. "It's been said," Obama told the audience, "that no one can ever truly understand what it's like being president until they sit behind that desk and feel the weight and responsibility for the first time. And that is true. After three and a half years in office—and much more gray hair—I have a deeper understanding of the challenges faced by the presidents who came before me, including my immediate predecessor, President Bush. In this job, no decision that reaches your desk is easy. No choice you make is without costs. No matter how hard you try, you're not going to make everybody happy. I think that's something President Bush and I both learned pretty quickly."

The Obamas at the Democratic National Convention 2008. "Yes We Can" by will.i.am was a viral sensation; the campaign had also used Brooks & Dunn's "Only in America."

With an ironic twinkle, Bush marked the moment with a bit of self-deprecation, or at least self-awareness: "I am also pleased, Mr. President," Bush said to Obama, "that when you are wandering these halls as you wrestle with tough decisions, you will now be able to gaze at this portrait and ask, 'What would George do?'"

History is full of examples of presidents thinking and talking about their predecessors, seeking inspiration or warning from the successes and the failures of those who came before. The enormity of that shared experience—of the feeling of holding ultimate power and ultimate responsibility—can create strange connections and alliances once the heat of battle has faded.

Bush and Obama shared something else: a song. In the fall of 1999, Kix Brooks and a few songwriting pals were on Brooks's farm in Tennessee, killing time. "After a good long day in the woods, we were sitting back at one of my cabins going on about how amazing it was that we could live a life like we live, just making words rhyme, and making up stories that people might care about," Brooks recalled. "At some point, I realized we were a couple of grown men just sitting around talking about how much we loved America. Sounds corny maybe, but we were feeling it, and I said, 'Man, we've got to write this thing.'" The result was "Only in America," which Brooks and his partner, Ronnie Dunn, soon recorded.

Brooks & Dunn performed the song at the preinaugural celebration for George W. Bush in 2001, and the forty-third president played "Only in America" as an anthem in the 2004 campaign. When Bush's team asked for the okay to use it at rallies, Brooks replied, "Well, of course; I'm always excited when someone likes my work." Reflecting on the song, Brooks said, "It was never meant to be political; it was patriotic, not partisan."

ONLY IN AMERICA

This Brooks & Dunn song, written by my fellow Louisiana native Kix Brooks, along with Don Cook and Ronnie Rogers, came out before 9/11 but was caught in the wave of songs that rolled in after the tragedy. Its universal message has allowed it to have an ongoing life and involvement in our political discourse through conventions and rallies. It is a fairly straightforward country track, building off major rock-guitar licks. It's musically uplifting.

Broken down lyrically, it is obvious in its messages of hopes and dreams—a common theme of many of the songs we've considered.

As a country founded on hopes and dreams and a better life, it seems fitting we close there. The universal message of "Only in America" contrasted

> with the themes of other songs that came out post–9/11. It's of the moment but not limited by it, and it will be sung for a long time coming.   —T.M.

That was clear in 2008, when Brooks and his wife, Barbara, were watching Barack Obama accept the Democratic nomination for president in Denver. The Black Eyed Peas' will.i.am had recorded "Yes We Can," a song punctuated with quotations from a memorable speech of Obama's in New Hampshire early in 2008; it was a viral success. But now, in Colorado, at the end of the evening, as the young Obama family stood on the stage, "Only in America" was suddenly reverberating through the stadium:

> Sun comin' up over New York City
> School bus driver in a traffic jam
> Staring out at the faces in a rearview mirror
> Lookin' at the promise of the Promised Land
> One kid dreams of fame and fortune
> One kid helps pay the rent
> One could end up going to prison
> One just might be president
> Only in America
> Dreamin' in red white and blue
> Only in America
> Where we dream as big as we want to
> We all get a chance
> Everybody gets to dance
> Only in America

There, briefly, in a time of warring camps, was a bit of common ground as two parties—two Americas, really—celebrated their competing visions of the future to the sound of the same song. A small thing, but in a dissonant world, every moment of harmony counts—and if we share music, we might just shout in anger a little less and sing in unity a bit more. Or so we can hope.

LIFT EVERY VOICE

Let America be the dream the dreamers dreamed.

—Langston Hughes

For thirteen hours at the White House on Monday, June 14, 1965, Lady Bird and Lyndon Johnson hosted several hundred guests at an elaborate Festival of the Arts. "Our painting and music, architecture and writing, have profoundly shaped the course of modern art," President Johnson told the gathering. "From jazz and folk song to the most complex abstractions of word and image, few parts of the world are free from the spreading influence of American culture. I do not pretend to judge the lasting values of these works. But if art is important to man, then American art is deeply important to mankind."

America being America, and artists being artists, the day was not without controversy. The poet Robert Lowell had declined the Johnsons' invitation and then publicly denounced the administration for its policy in Vietnam, among other foreign-policy issues; the critic Dwight Macdonald tried to have it both ways, showing up for the festival but seeking signatures for an anti-Johnson statement. Ralph Ellison, whose award-winning novel *Invisible Man* spoke to the social and intellectual issues faced by Black Americans in the early twentieth century, was underwhelmed by the petition drive, such as it was, dismissing it

Duke Ellington at the White House Festival of the Arts, Monday, June 14, 1965.

with a single word: *adolescent.* The Kennedy-Johnson adviser and speechwriter Richard Goodwin told Macdonald that the on-site agitation was "the height of rudeness." Charlton Heston, the star of *Ben-Hur* and *The Ten Commandments,* may have put it most vividly, remarking, "He belts me in his movie reviews. Why should I sign his lousy petition?" Macdonald collected fewer than ten names. "The others," *Time* noted, "were either embarrassed or outraged."

Johnson was unhappy about the dissonant voices, but he sought to make the best of things by staking out the high ground. "Your art is not a political weapon," the president said. "Yet much of what you do is profoundly political. For you seek out the common pleasures and visions, the terrors and the cruelties, of man's day on this planet. And I would hope that you would help dissolve the barriers of hatred and ignorance which are the source of so much of our pain and danger. In this way you work toward peace—not only the peace which is simply the absence of war but the peace which liberates man to reach for the finest fulfillment of his spirit." It was, really, the best—and only—thing the president could say in a moment of dissent.

Toward the end of the festival, as evening came, Marian Anderson introduced a musical program in the State Dining Room, noting that "strong, firm, young American voices" were now being heard across Europe. The audience then listened to Roberta Peters of the Metropolitan Opera sing "Glitter and Be Gay" from Leonard Bernstein's *Candide* and "Summertime" from George Gershwin's *Porgy and Bess.* The Joffrey Ballet performed after remarks by Gene Kelly.

Then Duke Ellington and his orchestra took the stage, and the tension of the day dissipated somewhat. He opened with "Take the 'A' Train." "Ties were loosened, shoes and jackets came off," the conductor Maurice Peress recalled. "I remember smiles and dancing. We were caught in the delicious, delirious embrace of Duke's music." Ellington played the "Black" movement of his symphony about the African American experience, *Black, Brown and Beige.* The composition included "Come Sunday," a spiritual. "God of love," the lyrics read, "please look down and see my people through."

In 1941, Ellington had delivered a speech that took as its text Langston Hughes's poem "I, Too." "I contend that the Negro is the creative voice of America, is creative America," Ellington had said then. "We stirred in our shackles and our unrest awakened Justice in the hearts of a courageous few, and we re-created in America the desire for true democracy, freedom for all, the brotherhood of man, principles on which the country had been founded." Those principles are eternal, but so is the war to make them concrete in the life of the nation.

It's a war without end. In the first decades of the twenty-first century, we find ourselves in a dispiriting moment in which what Ellington called "the brotherhood of man" is at best elusive and at worst out of reach. Many, if not most, Americans say they think the country is on the wrong track, and their faith in the future is tenuous. A common theme—*the* common theme, really, of the public conversation about America at the moment—is succinct and sad: We are divided as rarely, if ever, before, and the ferocious partisanship of the age lies at the heart of our discontent.

Many of the forces in evidence in our time, though, are not new. Nativism, xenophobia, cultural populism, and broad political fear have shaped the republic from the beginning and likely always will. Anxiety and its manifestations in the public square ebb and flow—and, truth be told, they mostly flow.

Given the current state of the nation, can music play any role in smoothing out the sharp edges of our disagreements and easing the tensions of tribalism?

History suggests it can. There's something about the transporting capacity of music, something about its odd but undeniable ability to create a collective experience by firing our individual imaginations, that's more likely to open our minds and our hearts to competing points of view. Music can recast the most charged and complicated of issues in ways that may lead to actual conversation rather than reflexive confrontation.

America is about debate, dissent, and dispute. We're always arguing, always fighting, always restless—and our music is a mirror and a maker of that once and future truth. "The Liberty Song" vs. "The Rebels"; "The Battle Hymn of the Republic" vs. "I Wish I Was in Dixie's Land"; "Happy Days Are Here Again" vs. "Brother, Can You Spare a Dime?"; "The Ballad of the Green Berets" vs. "Fortunate Son"; "Born in the U.S.A." vs. "God Bless the U.S.A.": The whole panoply of America can be traced—and, more important, *heard* and *felt*—in the songs that echo through our public squares. And if we can *hear* and *feel* how the other guys hear and feel, we're better equipped to press on toward a more perfect union.

For the song of America is not finished; the last notes have not yet been played. In that spirit, in that cause, now and always, let us lift every voice, and sing.

ACKNOWLEDGMENTS

JON MEACHAM

This project began, really, in my yard in Nashville. On an unseasonably warm winter afternoon, my friend and neighbor Tim McGraw suggested that we team up to tell the story of the nation not only through words (my part) but through music (his, which I probably don't need to point out). I had just published a book, *The Soul of America: The Battle for Our Better Angels,* about how the nation often gets big stuff wrong but can, at times, rise above its baser instincts. Why not explore that national soul, Tim asked, through music?

I was in. The result is the book you're reading.

We are grateful to several members of the academic community for their kindness and assistance; each graciously read all or parts of the manuscript amid busy lives and demanding schedules. (They bear no responsibility for the final product, of course; that's on us.) Craig Werner, professor of Afro-American Studies at the University of Wisconsin and the author of several essential books (among them *A Change Is Gonna Come: Music, Race, and the Soul of America* and *We Gotta Get Out of This Place: The Soundtrack of the Vietnam War,* written with Doug Bradley), was a judicious and invaluable reader. Michael Eric Dyson, University Professor of Sociology at Georgetown University and Renaissance man, guided us on the question of hip-hop. Imani Perry, the Hughes-Rogers Professor of African-American Studies at Princeton University, is a scholar of many things, and we drew on her wisdom about James Weldon Johnson's "Lift Every Voice and Sing," the subject of her book *May We Forever Stand: A History of the Black National Anthem.* David Blight, Class of 1954 Professor of American History and Director of the Gilder Lehrman Center for the Study of Slavery, Resistance, and Abolition at Yale University, was generous on Frederick Douglass, the subject of

David's recent (and marvelous) biography, *Frederick Douglass: Prophet of Freedom*. Christian McWhirter, Lincoln Historian at the Abraham Lincoln Presidential Library and Museum in Springfield, Illinois, and the author of the terrific *Battle Hymns: The Power and Popularity of Music in the Civil War*, read and commented on the Civil War sections. And as ever, Michael Beschloss is a devoted and selfless friend.

Will Byrd was invaluable in keeping the authors in good order; he is a steadfast friend and counselor. CAA's Rachel Adler, Cait Hoyt, and Kate Childs are a superb team. At Random House—my publishing home for just about two decades—I am, as always, grateful to the marvelous Kate Medina, Erica Gonzalez, Dennis Ambrose, Avideh Bashirrad, Benjamin Dreyer, Rebecca Berlant, Porscha Burke, Simon Sullivan (for the beautiful design of the book), Paolo Pepe (for the wonderful jacket), Karen Fink, Mary Moates, Maria Braeckel, Susan Corcoran, Leigh Marchant, Barbara Fillon, Andrea DeWerd, Katie Tull, Carol Poticny (for splendid photo research), and Kathy Lord (for her copyedit of the manuscript). And Gina Centrello remains the best of publishers and of friends—a tough combination, but she pulls it off with remarkable grace and skill.

John Lewis, Michael Eric Dyson, Sig Rogich, and Kix Brooks took time to share thoughts and recollections with us; we are hugely grateful. Doris Kearns Goodwin, Quincy Jones, and Ken Burns were generous with their time and their formidable talents. As noted, I drew on several existing essays of mine for sections of the book, and I am grateful to my editors at the *New York Times*, particularly Clay Risen; at *Time*; and at *Newsweek*. *Time*'s Anna Rumer in Washington contributed reporting to the essay on the fortieth anniversary of the death of Elvis Presley, and I fondly remember working with Vern E. Smith and Veronica Chambers on a *Newsweek* project commemorating the thirtieth anniversary of Martin Luther King, Jr.'s death. And Maynard Parker, Mark Whitaker, Evan Thomas, Howard Fineman, Ann McDaniel, Mark Miller, and Tom Watson each played roles in allowing me to write the 2004 remembrance of Ronald Reagan that we drew on to discuss the 1980s. My thanks to them all.

This book would not have been possible without the tireless, insightful, and cheerful assistance of Mike Hill. This is our seventh project together, and my debt to Mike is incalculable. Merrill Fabry checked the manuscript with care and intelligence; our thanks to her. Charles Robinson and Brad Joe of the Choctaw Nation of Oklahoma kindly provided us with a Choctaw song and its translation. In Nashville, Bill Lloyd offered the benefit of years of experience in the music business. Roxanne Oldham was essential in the tricky work of obtaining permissions for the quoted song lyrics, as was Evan Rosenblum. Margaret Shannon, longtime historian at Washington National Cathedral, was always on call. And Jack Bales is secure in his standing as the nation's finest bibliographer.

For courtesies small and large, thanks to Amanda Urban, Oscie and Evan Thomas, Nick Zeppos, Beth and John Geer, Julia Reed, Callie Khouri, Beth Laski, James Ring Adams, Sean Wilentz, Karl Rove, Katie Hill, and Eddie Glaude, Jr.

This book is dedicated to two daughters of Mississippi, Keith Meacham and Faith Hill. For me, as always, Mary, Maggie, and Sam are the *de facto* dedicatees. They are the center of everything, even if they have been particularly merciless in their opinions about their father's musical abilities (or lack thereof). They call 'em as they see 'em—or, in keeping with the spirit of this book, *hear* 'em.

TIM McGRAW

How can we know where we are going without some perspective on where we have been? That's why history fascinates me—it's the *story* of what made us a people and a nation. And telling stories is at the heart of what I'm always trying to do onstage or in a studio. The "Songs of America" project, then, is a piece of what I've spent so much of my life doing: taking the raw material of life and weaving it together into what I hope is something that not only entertains but illuminates.

My life as an artist has allowed me to meet some of the most amazing people in the world. It has given me a chance to look into their lives through meaningful conversation, gaining perspective and understanding. Sometimes these encounters are with a hope of taking away something that I will incorporate into a performance of some kind but always with the desire to learn and be better in my life.

One of those people is Jon Meacham. Out of our conversations together over the past few years the idea for this book was born. We were both enchanted by the fact that interwoven into the fabric of our national story were songwriters and performers creating lyrics and melodies at times of great challenge. From forming the country itself to overcoming the economic hardship of the Great Depression to fighting for rights, civil and otherwise, songs have told us much, and still do.

Music can give you a respite from the grind of life, to find an escape so that you can unwind from the pressures of life. But it can also shape and transform people and countries. When America was being founded and developed, artists— writers and performers—were in the moment. They were either leading with their writings or reflecting the sentiment of the population. Think of this: As our country was being formed, the writers of the day were as close in time to the era of Shakespeare as they were to our own age. We as songwriters are always trying to put into words what someone else is thinking. Empowering them.

Partnering with Jon has allowed me to voice some of my thoughts and ideas in the context of our American history. In these pages, I hope you can feel my passion for this country and my belief that we can continue to evolve and change and be better. I hope you can feel that in my music as well. And if my celebrity can be of any influence, I'd use it to encourage you to dig in and read and explore more about our incredible nation and its music. If you have interest in an era or a song, go further: read more books, listen to every version of the song, ask your friends or family. There are more songs and historical moments we just couldn't get to, and we certainly don't want to imply that this is a comprehensive effort. I encourage all of you to do your own research and learn more about the crossroads of history and music in our country. Find other songs. When you are digging into history, keep music and its role and influence in mind. Mine down into the different musical versions of the songs we've highlighted and discover how they have been adapted musically, but also see how they have been adapted in terms of patriotism or protest or politics.

I want to thank the readers for going on this journey of history and music with us. I hope you've enjoyed a deeper look into the intersection of the sounds and sagas of America. Knowledge is power and we hope to empower you to want to learn more.

Thanks to my team, especially Scott Siman and Kelly Clague, for being sounding boards and helping me flesh out my ideas for the song critiques. I am grateful to Random House for believing in this project and to everyone there for all your hard work to bring it to life. And a special thanks to Will Byrd for helping to keep us on the right track at the right time.

IMAGE CREDITS

xii–1: The 1914 restoration of the Star-Spangled Banner that inspired Francis Scott Key: BETTMANN/ GETTY IMAGES • 2: *The Nation Makers,* by Howard Pyle, 1903: NATIONAL MUSEUM OF AMERICAN ILLUSTRATION, NEWPORT, RI, AND AMERICAN ILLUSTRATORS GALLERY, NEW YORK, NY/BRIDGEMAN IMAGES • 6: *Writing the Declaration of Independence, 1776,* by Jean Leon Gerome Ferris, first half of the twentieth century: VIRGINIA MUSEUM OF HISTORY & CULTURE (1996.49.15) • 12: Burning of Stamp Act, Boston, Massachusetts, 1765: NIDAY PICTURE LIBRARY/ALAMY STOCK PHOTO • 12: *O! The Fatal Stamp,* published in *Pennsylvania Journal,* 1765: GLASSHOUSE IMAGES/EVERETT COLLECTION • 14: *Spirit of '76,* by Archibald Willard, 1898: THE STAPLETON COLLECTION/BRIDGEMAN IMAGES • 16: *Declaration of Independence,* by John Trumbull, 1818: ARCHITECT OF THE CAPITOL • 17: Portrait of Thomas Jefferson by Rembrandt Peale, 1805: COLLECTION OF THE NEW-YORK HISTORICAL SOCIETY, USA/BRIDGEMAN IMAGES • 17: Portrait of John Adams by Gilbert Stuart, circa 1800–1815: ARTOKOLORO QUINT LOX LIMITED/ALAMY STOCK PHOTO • 17: Portrait of Abigail Adams by Mather Brown, 1785: SCIENCE HISTORY IMAGES / ALAMY STOCK PHOTO • 21: *Poems on Various Subjects, Religious and Moral,* by Phillis Wheatley, 1773: BRITISH LIBRARY, LONDON, UK/© BRITISH LIBRARY BOARD. ALL RIGHTS RESERVED/BRIDGEMAN IMAGES • 28: Sheet music cover of the song "Hail, Columbia!," 1898: SHERIDAN LIBRARIES/LEVY/GADO/GETTY IMAGES • 30: 1814 burning of the White House by the British army during the War of 1812: NORTH WIND PICTURE ARCHIVES/AP IMAGES • 32: Naval battle during War of 1812 between the U.S. frigate *Constitution* and the British warship *Guerriere,* 1812: EVERETT COLLECTION • 33: General Andrew Jackson's victory at the 1815 Battle of New Orleans, illustration circa 1889: POPPERFOTO/GETTY IMAGES • 34: Star-Spangled Banner flag: DIVISION OF ARMED FORCES HISTORY, NATIONAL MUSEUM OF AMERICAN HISTORY, SMITHSONIAN INSTITUTION • 35: Francis Scott Key's handwritten manuscript of "The Star-Spangled Banner," 1814: GRANGER • 35: The first printed sheet music edition of Francis Scott Key's "The Star-Spangled Banner," Baltimore, 1814: SARIN IMAGES/GRANGER • 41: Illustration of Samuel Francis Smith and his lyrics to the song "America": USED WITH PERMISSION FROM THE COLLECTIONS OF THE NEWTON FREE LIBRARY, MASSACHUSETTS • 45: *Trail of Tears,* by Brummett Echohawk, 1957: 0227.1487, BRUMMETT ECHOHAWK, NATIVE AMERICAN ARTIST; PAWNEE, 1957, GILCREASE MUSEUM, TULSA, OKLAHOMA • 47: "The Liberator William Lloyd Garrison abolitionist" banner, American School, 1831: MASSACHUSETTS HISTORICAL SOCIETY, BOSTON, MA, USA/BRIDGEMAN IMAGES • 48: *Walker's Appeal,* by David Walker (1829), second edition, 1830: F&A ARCHIVE/ART RESOURCE, NY • 53: Harriet Tubman portrait by Harvey B. Lindsley, circa 1870s: LIBRARY OF CONGRESS PRINTS AND PHOTOGRAPHS DIVISION, WASHINGTON, D.C., REPRODUCTION NUMBER: LC-USZ62-7816 • 58: Frederick Douglass, circa 1855: EVERETT COLLECTION • 66: President Lincoln and General George B. McClellan following the Battle of Antietam, photograph by Alexander Gardner, 1862: EVERETT COLLECTION • 67: Text of the Emancipation Proclamation, 1888: UNIVERSAL

HISTORY ARCHIVE/UIG/BRIDGEMAN IMAGES • 70: Julia Ward Howe, author of the lyrics for "Battle Hymn of the Republic," circa 1906: CSU ARCHIVES/EVERETT COLLECTION • 71: Sheet music cover of the song "Battle Hymn of the Republic," 1898: SHERIDAN LIBRARIES/LEVY/GADO/GETTY IMAGES • 77: Sheet music cover of the song "I Wish I Was in Dixie's Land," 1860: SHERIDAN LIBRARIES/LEVY/GADO/GETTY IMAGES • 77: Daniel Decatur Emmett, who wrote the song "Dixie": © CORBIS/GETTY IMAGES • 79: Sheet music cover of the song "The Bonnie Blue Flag," 1864: GADO IMAGES/ALAMY STOCK PHOTO • 81: List of "Patriotic Songs," 1888: SHERIDAN LIBRARIES/LEVY/GADO/GETTY IMAGES • 86: Susan B. Anthony and Elizabeth Cady Stanton, 1895: USED WITH THE PERMISSION OF THE NATIONAL SUSAN B. ANTHONY MUSEUM & HOUSE • 89: Women suffragettes holding a banner addressing President Woodrow Wilson, Washington, D.C., 1917: GRANGER • 91: Suffrage Parade on Fifth Avenue, 1915: BETTMANN/GETTY IMAGES • 93: W. E. B. Du Bois: SCIENCE HISTORY IMAGES/ALAMY STOCK PHOTO • 94: Niagara Movement in Fort Erie, Canada, 1905: EVERETT COLLECTION • 95: Group portrait of composers Bob Cole, James Weldon Johnson, and J. Rosamond Johnson, circa 1900s: SCHOMBURG CENTER FOR RESEARCH IN BLACK CULTURE, PHOTOGRAPHS AND PRINTS DIVISION, THE NEW YORK PUBLIC LIBRARY Digital Collections http://digitalcollections.nypl.org/items/7f947850-e020-0130-79c8-58d385a7b928 • 96–97: Twentieth annual session of the NAACP, Cleveland, Ohio, 1929: EVERETT COLLECTION/ALAMY STOCK PHOTO • 99: U.S. soldiers in World War I, at the Western Front, Dieffmatten, Alsace, France: © HULTON-DEUTSCH COLLECTION/CORBIS/GETTY IMAGES • 101: Sheet music cover of the song "You're a Grand Old Flag," 1906: SHERIDAN LIBRARIES/LEVY/GADO/GETTY IMAGES • 101: Sheet music cover of the song "Over There," 1918: UNIVERSAL HISTORY ARCHIVE/UIG/GETTY IMAGES • 103: Sheet music cover of the song "I Didn't Raise My Boy to Be a Soldier/A Mother's Plea for Peace," 1915: GADO IMAGES/ALAMY STOCK PHOTO • 105: Katharine Lee Bates, who wrote the words to "America the Beautiful": BACHRACH/GETTY IMAGES • 109: Marian Anderson giving an Easter concert at the Lincoln Memorial, 1939: THOMAS D. MCAVOY/THE LIFE PICTURE COLLECTION/GETTY IMAGES • 110: Irving Berlin at the piano surrounded by American soldiers: BETTMANN/GETTY IMAGES • 113: Franklin D. Roosevelt, governor of New York, at the Democratic convention in Chicago, 1932: BETTMANN/GETTY IMAGES • 115: "The Bread Line" poster, printed by the National Service Bureau, circa 1920s: DAVID POLLACK/CORBIS/GETTY IMAGES • 117: A large dust cloud appears behind a truck traveling on Highway 59, south of Lamar, Colorado, May 1936: PHOTOQUEST/ARCHIVE PHOTOS/GETTY IMAGES • 118: Woodrow Wilson "Woody" Guthrie, 1950: UNIVERSAL HISTORY ARCHIVE/BRIDGEMAN IMAGES • 120: Eleanor Roosevelt with Marian Anderson in Japan, May 22, 1953: COURTESY OF THE FRANKLIN D. ROOSEVELT PRESIDENTIAL LIBRARY AND MUSEUM, HYDE PARK, NEW YORK • 124: "Never was so much owed by so many to so few," circa 1941: MARY EVANS PICTURE LIBRARY/EVERETT COLLECTION • 126: Vera Lynn serves tea to servicemen from the YMCA canteen, Trafalgar Square, London, 1942: KEYSTONE/HULTON ARCHIVE/GETTY IMAGES • 127: President Franklin Roosevelt and Prime Minister Winston Churchill singing hymns during the Divine Service on board HMS *Prince of Wales,* August 1941: BIRMINGHAM POST AND MAIL ARCHIVE/MIRRORPIX/GETTY IMAGES • 129: Sheet music cover of the song "We'll Meet Again," by Ross Parker and Hughie Charles,

SONG LYRIC CREDITS

INDEX

ABOUT THE AUTHORS

JON MEACHAM is a Pulitzer Prize-winning biographer. The author of the *New York Times* bestsellers *Thomas Jefferson: The Art of Power; American Lion: Andrew Jackson in the White House; Franklin and Winston; Destiny and Power: The American Odyssey of George Herbert Walker Bush;* and *The Soul of America,* Meacham holds the Carolyn T. and Robert M. Rogers Chair in the American Presidency and is a distinguished visiting professor at Vanderbilt University. He is a contributing writer to *The New York Times Book Review,* a contributing editor to *Time,* and a fellow of the Society of American Historians.

TIM McGRAW is a Grammy Award–winning entertainer, author, and actor who has sold more than 85 million records worldwide and dominated the charts with a stunning 45 number-one singles on country radio. He is one of the most played country artists on radio since his debut in 1992 and has three *New York Times* bestselling books to his credit. He has acted in such movies as *Friday Night Lights* and *The Blind Side* and in the television series *1883.* McGraw is considered one of the most successful touring acts in the history of country music. He has brought to life some of the biggest hit songs of all time, including "Live Like You Were Dying" and "Humble and Kind," with messages that continue to impact fans around the world.